MC

Disfigured

Disfigured

A SAUDI WOMAN'S STORY OF TRIUMPH OVER VIOLENCE

by Rania Al-Baz
translated by Catherine Spencer

OLIVE
BRANCH
PRESS

An imprint of Interlink Publishing Group, Inc.
www.interlinkbooks.com

First published in 2009 by

OLIVE BRANCH PRESS
An imprint of Interlink Publishing Group, Inc.
46 Crosby Street, Northampton, MA 01060
www.interlinkbooks.com

Originally published in French as *Défigurée: Quand un crime passionnel devient affaire d'État.*

To protect their privacy, the names of the people in this story have been changed.

Library of Congress Cataloging-in-Publication Data
Al-Baz, Rania.
[Défigurée. English]
Disfigured : a Saudi woman's story of triumph over violence / by Rania al-Baz; translated by Catherine Spencer.—1st American ed.
    p. cm.
ISBN 978-1-56656-735-0 (pbk.)
1. Al-Baz, Rania. 2. Abused wives—Saudi Arabia—Biography. 3. Women television journalists—Saudi Arabia—Biography. 4. Muslim women—Saudi Arabia—Social conditions. 5. Women—Saudi Arabia—Social conditions.
6. Family-violence—Saudi Arabia. I. Title.
HQ1730.Z75A4413 2005
362.82'92092—dc22   [B]
                     20080154

Printed and bound in the United States of America

To request our complete 40-page full-color catalog, please call us toll free at 1-800-238-LINK, visit our website at www.interlinkbooks.com, or write to Interlink Publishing, 46 Crosby Street, Northampton, MA 01060
email: info@interlink books.com

To my friend Joseph Kassis, who has been my guiding light during this long, dark night. The waves of his tenderness have washed over the wounds of my life. I dedicate my present to him, for him to share with my friend Roda.

Death on the Horizon

Light. Quick!—the light. My shaking hand gropes the bedside table, feeling for the switch. Finally, I find it. A soft light fills the bedroom and I look around, my eyes lingering over every piece of furniture. I have to convince myself that they're really there. My heart is beating wildly, my breathing rapid, my nightgown covered with sweat; I can feel icy droplets running down my entire body.

Mechanically I pass my hand over my eyes, my face. I am well and truly alive: it was nothing but a nightmare. I sit up slowly, leaning back on the pillow to calm myself. Lying next to me, my husband stirs a little, turns to face the wall, grunts, and then goes back to sleep. I remain motionless for several minutes, then turn out the light and slip back under the thin sheet. But I don't want to sleep. It's the last thing I want. I'm too frightened of being plunged again into the horrific dream. I look at my husband. I don't want him there beside me; the dream frightened me, but he terrifies me. The images still parade through my head, engraved in my mind:

I cannot get rid of them. They are written into the darkness and the silence of the night.

I was stretched out on the ground, stiff and frozen, while thousands of ants crawled over my body. I could feel them and see them advancing toward my face, my eyes, my mouth; I tried to scream but no sound emerged. I was going to be swallowed up by this swarming tide that nothing could stop. It was advancing relentlessly when suddenly my aunt Nefta appeared above me. She plunged her hands into that unspeakable mass and pulled me up toward the sky.

This unexpected rescue should have put an end to my torment. Should have... but in fact when I awoke, I only grew more anxious. The dream had been so heavy with significance and so charged with bad omens. I am, of course, a believer. I know that there is life after death. In Islam, dreams can be interpreted, but they shouldn't be confused with visions. Only prophets can have visions—the most famous being that of Joseph and his seven cows.

Joseph was very handsome and the king's wife tried to seduce him. He refused her advances, however, and was duly thrown into prison. He was known for his talent for interpreting dreams and one day was asked to interpret one of the king's dreams, in which seven fat cows ate seven thin cows. Joseph declared that seven years of drought would follow seven years of plenty. The king organized the saving and storing of crops throughout the land and when Joseph's predictions came true, the kingdom was well prepared for the disaster, and Joseph was freed by the grateful king. And this is why we believe in the interpretation of dreams.

This aunt who had descended from the sky in my dream had died several years earlier. Muslims believe that when someone, even a benevolent figure, who has departed takes us by the hand in a dream, it means we will soon join them in the hereafter.

Despite the affection I felt for my deceased aunt, at 29 years old this prospect scared me. I couldn't stop thinking about it, with a heavy sense of anxiety—first because I had been brought up with these beliefs, which I respect, and then because this wretched dream came at a time when I was already full of doubt, questioning my whole life and future. I seemed to be at an impasse; I felt unhappy, despairing, even though it was clear to me that the Almighty was carving out my path. He had come to help me by showing me the most noble and generous way out of my sorrow; He was showing me the path that led to Him.

I had not yet thought of the supreme solution of death, and yet at the same time I felt that my existence no longer had much meaning. Everything seemed black. Every day I fell a little deeper into hell, certain that no one and nothing could pull me out. Despite my youth, I was already profoundly marked by an unusual story and by a succession of catastrophes.

I had been divorced before I was eighteen. Even in the West, where divorce is permitted and no one is shocked by it, it is still remarked upon. It is seen, however, as a failure rather than as something morally degrading—a regrettable misfortune of life rather than an indelible stain. But in the East, it is a completely different matter. A divorced woman is a repudiated woman who has failed to satisfy her husband and to keep her place as spouse, mother, and mistress of the house. People point to her in the street. She is suspected of every kind of wrong. She cannot be trusted.

I was born in Mecca, where my grandfather was a notable figure. Mecca is the guarantor of our religion's rules and laws, the obligatory destination for pilgrimage, the site of the mosque where the Prophet was buried, and the repository of the sacred Black Stone, the Ka'aba. Imagine, then, how difficult it is for a divorced woman to live in this place of tradition and conformity, where the purest version of the Qur'an is rigorously guarded!

So I took my divorce very hard. I experienced it as a humiliation and, above all, as an affront to my family. I felt incredibly guilty. It took me a long time and much affection to get over this separation. I was convinced that it had condemned me to live alone for the rest of my life and for me this was nothing more than divine justice—the price to pay for the sin I had committed before the Creator. Before I could go on with my life, I had to accept my destiny with resignation—and I did accept it.

Undoubtedly, my looks, which were said to be rather agreeable, helped me to overcome my disgraced position. While studying radiology (without great conviction), with the guidance of a friend of my father's, I managed to become a newscaster on Channel 1, the Saudi public channel. Only a few older women had held this post before me; a twenty-year-old newscaster who took on rather lively topics was something totally new. And so my appearances on the small screen did not go unnoticed. It was a revolution that had the whole country talking. My celebrity attracted men and I was approached all day long. To my great surprise, they were falling over each other to ask my father for my hand in marriage, without worrying about my previous matrimonial misadventure. In such a situation, I found another husband quickly. Too quickly.

Rachid, a singer, proclaimed himself madly in love with me. He pestered my father to give his agreement to our marriage and eventually won him over. Rachid had also been married. I had a daughter aged five, Rahaf, and Rachid had three girls as well as an eight-year-old son. The boy would live with us, as would one of his sisters—an arrangement I accepted without, of course, my opinion having been asked.

As time passed, my husband's passionate love transmuted into an unhealthy, constant, oppressive, and unbearable jealousy. I was his possession, an object that he wanted to keep hidden away. He didn't lock me in the house, as some men in Saudi Arabia do, but he forbade me from seeing anyone, even my female friends. As for men—don't even mention it... Aside from my television appearances, I was practically shut away and under constant surveillance.

I had hoped that the birth of our first child, Saoud, would calm him down, but I was fooling myself. The arrival of our first son didn't change anything—nor did the arrival of the second, Nayef, two years later. Rachid only suffocated me more and more. In fact, he would have liked me to have a whole troop of children, to keep me tied to the house. He repeatedly asked me for more children, knowing that the more babies I had, the less capable I would be of resisting him in any way. He tolerated my continuing to work in television, and offered that as proof of his great openness and generosity. What a joke! It was our only source of income. His artistic career had come to an end and he had not put up for long with the pen-pushing job in the Jeddah chamber of commerce, procured for him by a friend. And so I had to work to support the family.

I did it willingly, without grumbling or complaining, just as I forced myself to be an attentive wife and mother. It was I who bought Rachid's clothes and furniture for the house. I sewed and made delicious little dishes for my husband's many guests. Even his sister acknowledged—with a touch of jealousy—that I was an exceptional cook. But my only reward was to be suspected of the worst intentions and placed under permanent high security. This injustice, so hard to bear, revolted me and yet I complied with all my husband's demands, like a good Muslim wife. A woman in my country has an absolute duty to look after her home, even if it means giving up her work. I held down both roles, as well as looking after my figure and my physical appearance with great perfectionism; this was rare in Saudi Arabia and only served to heighten Rachid's possessiveness.

I was alone in carrying this burden, which seemed to get heavier every day, crushing and breaking me. Sometimes I wanted to confide in my mother, but even the thought of telling her what my daily reality was made me feel I would die of shame.

Even my faithful friend Solina knew nothing. I stopped myself from sharing the least confidence with her because I didn't intend to tell her how I was treated and show her that, in the end, I had worse luck than her, despite my star status. Supposedly marital bullying was reserved for poor people. So I spoke of the truth of my life to no one. I was too scared that what I said would get back to Rachid.

I couldn't imagine his reaction—or, rather, I could imagine it only too well. Several times already, when I dared rebel, I had been on the receiving end of stinging slaps. If Rachid learned that I was portraying him as a bad husband to our friends, I knew what I could expect—so I was silent, waiting for the better days that I now hardly believed would come. It was safer. But in any case, there was no need for me to complain or talk about my life since Rachid was about to unmask himself in front of Solina.

One evening I was in bed, chatting on the phone to my friend, as I very often did, when my husband suddenly burst in. He was very excited and stared at me intently. I could see that a storm was about to erupt and I immediately interrupted my conversation with Solina: "Excuse me a minute, I think Rachid wants to talk to me..." Then, placing the telephone on my chest, I asked my husband gently, "Do you need something?"

I had hardly finished my sentence when he pointed a furious finger at me: "Who are you talking to?"

"Solina—why?"

Enraged, Rachid rushed over and wrenched the receiver from my hands. Instinctively, I protected my face, somehow convinced he was going to hit me. But no: brusquely turning his back on me, he screamed at Solina, "You will stop calling Rania and I forbid her to call you. Is that understood?"

He then hung up sharply before turning toward me with a menacing air: "Did you hear what I said? No more phone calls. Not to Solina, or anybody..."

Sinking back into my pillow, I lay petrified, pulling the sheet up under my chin in a pathetic gesture of protection. Without daring to utter a single word, I watched with enormous relief as Rachid left the room. Then I stared incredulously at the telephone. To ban me from speaking to my friend... it was insane! These phone conversations with my women friends were my last means of communication with the outside world, of not being totally alone. To deprive me of them was monstrous. I felt suffocated with rage. I wanted to scream, but my cries were strangled in my throat and instead a tide of tears suddenly spilled down my face. I had no choice. With us, it is the man who decides: he is the master and the woman can do nothing but obey. Rachid certainly did not seem deserving of the stature of a master but that changed nothing.

The following day, when Rachid was out, I braved the ban and called Solina to apologize, but as soon as she recognized my voice it was as though she were speaking to the devil: "Rania? Are you mad? Did you hear what your husband said? We mustn't call each other any more."

"But, Solina, it's ridiculous! I don't want to break off our friendship, whatever Rachid says."

"No, Rania, no, I don't want any trouble with your husband. He might complain to mine and we'd both be punished. Honestly, Rania, it's better for both of us. We'll meet up later, in a while, I promise you. Lots of love..."

Gently replacing the receiver, I had the horrible sensation that I was contagious with an invisible plague. My life was in tatters. I was disturbing everyone; I was not wanted. The terrible dream of the ants and my aunt coming to save me only upset me more. I was invaded by ideas of death. But wasn't I already dead to the world? Once again, I mentally implored my mother to come to my rescue. And still, I was unable to speak to her.

But I had to confide in someone and bear witness to a secret that was becoming much too heavy to carry. One way or another, I had to externalize it, or the ants of my dream would continue to devour me relentlessly. I could imagine those filthy insects gnawing my insides, sapping my vitality, drinking my blood, attacking my heart. I was certain I was going to die. My aunt would not have come into my dream for nothing. And so, one sad afternoon I took a white sheet of paper and began to write carefully, on the top right-hand side, these four words: "This is my will."

In the Islamic world, the tradition of writing one's will is inspired by the Prophet. I therefore started my task as if in prayer, without reflecting or realizing the impact of what I was writing: "If I am killed, I want you to pardon my murderer. Even if the murderer is my husband, do not demand reparation, because for my part I forgive."

This introduction was important for Islamic law is strict: killing is punishable by death and all aggressions or thefts are severely condemned. Only the victim can lessen the punishment if he or she wishes by offering forgiveness.

Why that specific allusion to my husband? I still cannot explain it. I swear that when I took the pen, I did not imagine for a single second that he would make an attempt on my life. And why that certainty that someone was going to kill me? Why talk about a crime rather than an accident? I think everything was being played out in my unconscious and that my words were dictated by a mixture of fear and resentment of my husband.

When I wrote my last wishes I was already in a state of psychological death; in that state, I found the rationale for my physical death. It was the normal, ordinary, and inevitable consequence of my psychic destruction. That was why neither an accident nor even an illness occurred to me. These misfortunes attack unexpectedly. As soon as they occur, they are perfectly identifiable and do not mask themselves. I felt death coming, but it was veiled and I had to guess what lay beneath. Since I essentially lived as a recluse, my murderer could only be one of my everyday companions. Apart from occasional visits to my family, I saw no one but my parents-in-law who lived just above us, my children, my husband and some of his carefully selected friends, and my colleagues, whom I encountered only during my working hours. I therefore had to identify my assassin from this small circle and it was the most natural thing in the world that my husband's name should impose itself without my even being aware of it.

But when I specified that my husband must "also" be forgiven, I had in my mind that it was "in the unlikely event that it was him." Which was of course unimaginable. The contradictions of despair...

My unconscious guessed the truth, yet consciously I lied to myself—or reassured myself. Perhaps both. Because in fact by writing "even if the murderer is my husband," I was pointing to him and broadcasting what was obvious: it could only be him. But it is hard to admit such a disturbing truth. I did not want to feel threatened by Rachid. For me, that would have been the acknowledgment of a second marital failure. Once more, I blamed myself.

I put my heart into the drawing up of my will, and mixed things and people, uniting the beings I loved with the most treasured objects, so as to be certain of handing over my most precious possessions—those to which I was the most attached, not necessarily the most expensive. For example, my mother had given one of my sisters and me each a watch and every time one of us traveled somewhere, we exchanged them, as a way of staying with each other, remaining in contact and thinking of each other. Remembering this ritual, I ordained that my beloved sister should inherit my watch.

Thinking of the hereafter was a strange sensation. I don't think I truly imagined I was going to die. The drafting of my will was above all a way of expressing my anxiety and of making an inventory of those I loved. I felt terribly alone and abandoned; I needed tenderness and affection. By this fictitious distribution of goods I made an account of all those whom I was certain cherished me. That comforted me.

After my nightmare, I decided to sleep in a separate room. I could no longer bear the idea of sleeping next to my husband. Something fundamental had broken for me. We could barely talk to each other and became like two shadows who were permanently trying to avoid each other. A status quo was established and each of us gave the impression of being content with it. But I am sure that it was only an apparent tranquility. I was well aware of a fire smoldering beneath the ashes, which I feared could surge up at any moment.

We remained entrenched in our positions for ten days, forcing ourselves to ignore each other. And then, one evening, Rachid came in when I was again talking on the phone to a woman friend. From his expression, I knew at once that the ceasefire was about to be broken and indeed, as soon as I hung up, the questions and threats began. But this time I defended myself; voices were raised. To end the argument, I went to sleep in my children's bed. Rachid did not follow me and went to bed himself.

Stretched out in the darkness, I could not sleep. I thought of the future: this situation could not continue. I had to find a solution. We couldn't go on like this for the rest of our days, nor live under the constant threat of such eruptions. After having thought for a long time, I decided to try once more for a reconciliation. Such an effort would hardly be easy, but I thought I had to make it for the sake of our relationship and our children.

Just after sunrise, I got up and went into the kitchen to prepare a hearty breakfast. I then set the table attractively for Rachid so that when he awoke he had only to sit down and serve himself tea. Once the scene was prepared, and I had satisfied myself one last time that everything was in order, I felt incredibly tired and went back to bed. The sudden wave of exhaustion made me drop to sleep like a rock.

I was still sound asleep when Rachid came in softly to wake me. I thought I was dreaming when I heard him murmuring gently in my ear before leaving. It was exquisite. I snuggled further into my pillow and went peacefully back to sleep.

When I woke, the apartment was deserted. I couldn't hear a sound. The children weren't there. Their beds were unmade; they must have gotten up in silence and gone with their father. This was an event; Rachid never took them with him. I began to hope: maybe my husband had also realized that we had to get out of this impasse and that doing so would require an effort from both of us. Had my carefully prepared breakfast had an effect? The few soft words that he had spoken to me before he left suggested that he had been in a good mood. His attitude was unusual, but not worrying. On the contrary, it displayed a new awareness and a desire to make peace.

This notion gave me renewed hope. Reassured, I took full advantage of the moment of serenity. The sitting room was bathed in warm sunshine and I stretched out on a sofa facing the window to enjoy it.

That day, April 4, 2004, I felt that I was living once more. I smiled at the thought of the will I had drawn up several days earlier and carefully hidden at the bottom of a drawer. Yet although it no longer seemed relevant, something stopped me from going to destroy it. Without worrying about it any further, I gave myself up to the well-being of that moment.

No news of Rachid or the children throughout the whole day. Not the briefest call. It was strange, but I didn't worry. Was Rachid finally discovering the joy of fatherhood? I profited from the calm by throwing myself into sewing; in order to save money, I designed, cut, and sewed my dresses myself. It was economical, but I also liked the work, and time always flew by when I was settled behind my sewing machine.

When I finally looked up from my pile of material, the sun had already gone down. Rachid had still not come back. This wasn't a concern, as outside the noise of the street grew louder, a reminder that in Saudi Arabia both towns and country villages get lively at night when the heat abates. As a performer, my husband was particularly nocturnal. He loved the nighttime. Little used to paternal responsibilities, he clearly didn't realize that it was rather late for the children and that they should long since have been in bed. But if it brought us peace, I excused him in advance for this breaking of their routine. While waiting for the return of my small family, I switched on the television to see what my friends on Channel 1 were showing.

Rachid and the children finally got back to the apartment shortly before midnight, making a ruckus as they arrived. Despite the late hour, the children were very excited. They rushed over to show me the presents their father had given them: superb little multicolored motorbikes that they immediately rode up and down the apartment in a concert of shouts and laughter. After several minutes, I interrupted their game and asked them to go to bed. It was past time.

Then I reflected on Rachid's behavior. It was good that he had treated his little ones, but I nonetheless asked myself how he could have paid for the toys. It irritated me a little when I knew that I had to juggle to make ends meet every month on a single salary. I said nothing, but it put me in a bad mood. I could not stop myself from being disagreeable when my husband came over to take a cigarette from my pack, without asking permission. It was idiotic but the gesture irritated me—as it always had—and I took the pack out of his hands.

"Leave my cigarettes. If you want, there are some in the kitchen."

I saw Rachid react angrily and march off to the other room; I immediately bit my lip. My spontaneous reaction had been stupid. It risked spoiling my good resolutions, and perhaps Rachid's—if he had made any. I had no more time to reflect on the issue because the telephone rang and I picked it up automatically, my eyes fixed on the kitchen door.

"Hello?"

"Yes, good evening, Rania. I'm just calling to see how you are."

I recognized the voice of my friend Leila. My heart skipped a beat. I could not control myself and interrupted her at once, "It's not a good time—I'll call you back…"

Too late. Rachid had already moved into the door frame and shot at me, "Who was it?"

"Leila."

Without a word, Rachid left the room, obviously furious, and went to watch television. I watched him go. I was sick of being treated like this and I wouldn't let it go on. Following my husband, I planted myself squarely in front of him, filled with an anger that was suffocating me, and erupted, "Rachid, that's it. Stop ruining my life. I made a mistake—I have never loved you. It's over. Get out of my life—"

Held in for too long, the words gushed out before I could stop them. Rachid fixed me with a black, piercing gaze and I felt his breath on my face. He yelled back, "And me? Do you think I love you? My poor girl, I only stay with you because of the children. Otherwise I would have left a long time ago!"

"Good! That's all right then, perfect, get out, and let's get a divorce—yes, a divorce. You go and live your life where you want and leave me alone."

Rachid was pale. He approached me again. Sensing danger and to protect myself from being hit, I issued the pathetic threat of a little girl, "If you hit me, I'll tell my father…"

I had gasped out the words. I was shaking and drew back, seeking to defend myself. I was terrified. Seizing me by the neck, Rachid spat in my face: "I am not going to hit you—I'm going to slit your throat."

Everything toppled around me. I was picked up from the ground and thrown back down against it, my face crashing against the white marble floor of the sitting room. A terrible pain invaded me, my head exploded, and I screamed; I couldn't see clearly and my eyes were full of blood. I made a desperate effort to get up, but Rachid was bearing down on me with his full force and I heard him say, in a guttural voice that I did not recognize, the words I will never forget: "Say your prayers, go on, say your prayers, you have time..."

And I said them! Yes, I said my Shahadah three times... I thought of death. Rachid again tightened the pressure around my neck and then the blows began, rapid and violent. He really wanted to kill me. I called the children, who were sleeping in their room, but as far as I knew, they were sound asleep and did not hear. I called for help but the neighbors did not come. A man beating up his wife is not so rare here; one doesn't get involved. It was over. I didn't struggle any more, but felt life slipping away as I lost consciousness.

What happened afterward? It took me several weeks to piece together the series of events, thanks to the evidence gathered by the police and the statements of my husband himself.

Rachid's rage was immediately replaced by panic. Suddenly realizing that he might have killed me, he got scared. His clothes were stained with blood, as were the walls and furniture around him. He quickly changed and then threw some belongings into a bag. He thought to take his passport—proof that he considered fleeing abroad—and then carried me to our car. He placed me in the back seat and drove me to a hospital four miles away. It was the middle of the night and the streets were deserted. Rachid left my body, unobserved by anyone, on the pavement in front of the hospital doors and then went to a hotel where his sister worked. She wasn't on duty, so he left his bag, saying he would come back later, and then disappeared.

I was found by a doctor leaving the hospital, only a few minutes after Rachid had abandoned me—fortunately, as I was losing a lot of blood. I was still unconscious and had no identification on me. Totally disfigured, I had no chance of being recognized even though my face was familiar to many television viewers.

I was immediately carried to the emergency room, while doctors tried to get me to talk, to keep me alive and to try to identify me.

I regained consciousness for a brief moment and was able, I was told, to whisper my name and a telephone number. Unluckily, it was that of my husband's cell phone and Rachid was obviously careful not to reply. He was not going to raise the alarm or tell my family that he had just tried to kill me. My rescuers therefore came back to me and, by I do not know what miracle, I managed this time to communicate my parents' number before lapsing definitively into a coma. It was two o'clock in the morning.

It was my sister who answered when the hospital called; she had gone down to get a glass of water in the kitchen when the phone rang. She had been frightened to pick up because my father had forbidden her from speaking on the phone after midnight, for fear that it would be a suitor. He didn't want his daughters to have any romantic attachments. "Be careful: no relationships with men," he always said. My sister had nonetheless answered eventually because she thought it might be bad news. She wasn't thinking of me; one of our brothers had recently had serious health problems and she feared hearing bad news about him. The shock was worse when she learned that I had just been hospitalized and that it was serious. They could not tell her more over the phone.

Several minutes later, my parents arrived at the hospital, but the doctors refused to let them go into the room where I was receiving intensive care, fearing that they would not be able to bear the shock of my disfigurement.

Meanwhile, the police had been alerted since the doctors were convinced that I had been attacked, and violently.

The revelation of my identity was like a bolt of lightning. The police had rushed over en masse when they received the call from the hospital. It was not every day that a television star got beaten up in their district.

Twelve police cars were already lined up outside the hospital when my parents arrived. Following the customary procedures, the detectives first asked my father a few basic questions, and my husband was quickly placed under suspicion.

After the interview, my mother suddenly lost her self-control and her nerves gave way. She demanded to see me and the doctors were obliged to give in. Fortunately, the bandages on my face hid the extent of the damage. The first X-rays showed thirteen fractures. I would have to undergo a first operation the following day, if my condition allowed for it. The doctors had warned my parents that they were uncertain of my chances of survival. Later they admitted that they had not placed them higher than three percent.

I managed to pull through, though, and I regained consciousness after four days in a coma. That terrible evening of April 4th then started to come back to me slowly and I felt immensely weary. I didn't even have the strength to be angry with Rachid. I wanted only two things: to sleep, and to forget.

I was unaware that the revelation of the attack had created a considerable storm throughout the country. My husband's crazed behavior had become an affair of state. The highest dignitaries condemned him. They worried about my health and demanded reparations. Completely unaware in my hospital bed, I didn't imagine for an instant that the photograph of my swollen face would go around the world and that my story would even be mentioned in the US Congress!

Everyone Rallies Around

From the moment I was identified, the hospital was in uproar. After I emerged from my days in a coma, doctors and nurses lined up at my bedside, all wanting to make sure that I wanted for nothing, that I wasn't in too much pain and that my condition was improving. I appreciated all their attention, but the ceaseless procession sometimes made me dizzy. I wanted calm and silence. Despite the drugs and the tranquilizers, stabbing pains regularly shot across my face, making me want to scream—but my cries were stifled by the bandages covering my lips; in my distress, I called out for my mother and asked her to comfort me. And then the pain died down and, calmed, I fell into short periods of sleep.

My first visits were authorized two days after I came out of the coma. My parents came immediately. My mother clung to the doctors, begging them to save my life while my father contented himself with raging against Rachid and the insult he had suffered at his hands. He had warned us...

He kept on repeating: "You see? I was right, I was right, and you were wrong!" Where did I figure in all this? I received neither a glance nor a word of compassion.

Then Hamuda, one of our neighbors and a friend of my father's, arrived. As soon as he set eyes on me, he burst into tears. He knew me well and knew what my life was like. Suddenly he caught hold of my father and shouted, "Rachid didn't kill her—you did! If you had been less severe, she would have come back to you a long time ago, and she wouldn't be in this state now!"

In my still semi-lethargic state, I heard all this as though it were part of a dream. I didn't recognize the voices and I understood nothing of what was going on; stupidly, I kept calling "Abi, Abi" [Daddy, Daddy]. I wanted, before I died, to entrust my children to him, to experience a real father, a tender father who would clasp me to him. But what could I hope for from the man who had kissed me just two or three times in nearly thirty years?

When I finally, and painfully, opened my eyes, I saw my mother and Hamuda at the foot of my bed. I later learned that Hamuda had stayed with my mother outside the door of my room the whole time I had been unconscious. Hamuda was in fact an old suitor. But he was Syrian and it had therefore been out of the question, as far as my father was concerned, for him to marry me. We are not allowed to marry foreigners. I knew that he had asked for my hand, but I didn't know that he loved me. When I made him out in my room—it still hurt to keep my eyelids open—instead of thanking him courteously for his presence, instinct overcame me and I blurted out, "You're the first person I see? What are you doing here?"

Totally disconcerted, the poor man mumbled, "Like everyone in the city, I've been very worried. I had to know how you were."

Those few words woke me up.

"People in the city are worried about me?"

My friend took hold of the lifeline I had just thrown him. "Yes, yes! People are talking about nothing else and the story of your attack is on the front page of all the newspapers."

Incredulous, I turned to my mother for confirmation.

"It's true," she said. "All the journalists wanted to see you and interview you but you aren't well enough yet. Above all, the doctors want you to rest. But the reporters are not far away: they're waiting outside the hospital for authorization to meet you. They ask us about your condition every time we go out. Yesterday, a policeman even found a photographer on the terrace of a nearby building—he had an enormous lens and was zooming in on all the rooms trying to find you!"

Listening to this, I slowly came to my senses. I knew nothing of what had happened since my attack. I didn't even know what had happened to my husband. My mother then filled me in on the chain of events.

After leaving me at the hospital and depositing a bag containing his things at the hotel where one of his sisters worked, Rachid had completely disappeared. No more news. No one knew where he was hiding. Because he had taken his passport, he might have succeeded in leaving the country, although the police believed that was unlikely and were actively looking for him. His photo had appeared in all the papers, which must have seriously impeded his chances of escape. There was no doubt that he would be captured sooner or later, which must give me some satisfaction.

And yet I felt nothing of the kind. My first reaction to the news clearly disconcerted my friends and family. While everyone expected me to demand justice and punishment, my mother's account terrified me; I imagined what was to me the worst case, which no one seemed to be considering. When Rachid saw the newspaper reports and realized the seriousness of what he had done, hunted and penniless (I knew he had no money), he might have committed suicide.

When I said this, a heavy silence fell over the room. No one had thought of this possibility and, above all, no one was worried about it. The fact that I, the victim, was concerned about it disconcerted the people gathered around my bed: my parents, my ex-suitor, and several other friends who had come. I knew what everyone was thinking but did not dare say: "Well, yes, it is possible. And so what? It wouldn't matter; he almost killed you."

But that was not how I felt. Rachid was the father of two of my children. Two children of whom, given the circumstances, I certainly would be given custody. What would they think of such a tragedy later in their lives? How would they understand it? Wouldn't I be partly responsible in their minds? After having lost their father, might they not reject their mother? It would be terrible for them and I didn't want that. Rachid was at fault in having attacked me, but it had taken both of us to get to that point of crisis. I wanted to reflect about it more, with a clear mind, and for that I needed to know my husband was alive; his death would falsify every judgment and would mark my life forever, condemning me, I feared, in the eyes of my two sons. I refused this horrible prospect, which would have been an unbearable agony for a mother. May Rachid be alive, live to recognize his wrong and take responsibility before our children. I wanted to leave them the possibility of judging him; I didn't want to do that for them.

For these reasons, the idea of my husband's possible death tortured me much more than my own condition. Still incapacitated, I couldn't make those around me understand that if Rachid were still alive, I wanted him to know that I forgave him. I even wanted to tell the judges immediately that I begged for their mercy. In the name of my children, I wanted to ask them not to sentence Rachid to ten years in prison, as the law allowed for such a crime, and even to spare him the 300 lashes in a public place set down in our criminal code. There too, I was thinking of our sons: such a spectacle would traumatize them. If I survived, I wanted to see them grow up in tranquility; I didn't want to inflict on them the vision of their father's public flagellation. I would ask the judges to hear my plea as soon as possible. A victim's requests for mercy are always taken into account in criminal judgments.

I saw only one way that my husband could know this: the press. Journalists would be my most effective messengers. Again I had to convince my nearest and dearest, who didn't seem at all taken with my idea. It didn't take me long to realize that they were remaining strangely silent. I didn't fully understand their reserve and embarrassment until one of my sisters, also present, commented, "Maybe you're still a bit too weak to see journalists; it would be better to wait a bit…"

I sat up in my bed as well as I could, while my mother rushed to prop up the pillows. I demanded brusquely, "Bring me a mirror!"

I had hit the nail on the head. There was immediate panic. The faces around me were aghast and everyone seemed to want the earth to swallow them; no one spoke.

I insisted, "It's not complicated. I want to see what I look like. I want to know how bad it is."

My mother was the first to break the silence. "I don't have a mirror with me. I'll go and ask a nurse…"

I knew she was lying. My mother was much too concerned about her appearance not to be carrying a mirror. I was certain now that I looked frightful, that I was disfigured and my face was nothing more than a living wound. I was filled with terrible anxiety.

Several minutes later, it was not a nurse but a doctor who came into the room. He came toward me smiling, his manner reassuring. "So, Rania, you want to see yourself? Today you won't see anything but bandages. We're going to start taking them off tomorrow. You can watch. It won't be a very pretty sight—you'll still have lots of bruises and wounds—but don't worry, we'll take care of all that later. You just need to be patient."

His speech did not convince me. Until then I had been in too much pain to think about my appearance. I knew that I was broken on the inside. Thirteen fractures was a lot for a single head. That had been more than enough to think about and I hadn't yet considered the external damage. I was now fully aware of it and I feared the moment of truth.

I had a difficult night. I had to take tranquilizers to sleep as I wondered again and again what I must look like. Despite the sleeping pills, I woke early and immediately demanded that my bandages be removed. The poor nurses tried to explain that they were waiting for the doctor and couldn't make any decisions without him, but it was no use: I raged and fumed against this wretched doctor who didn't come.

He finally showed up mid-morning to direct proceedings. With infinite care, the nurses began to unwind the bandages and remove the dressings. Their gestures were so slow that it felt as though the operation took hours, the nurses asking anxiously every moment, "Is that all right? We're not hurting you?"

When their work was done, the doctor approached and touched my face. Before handing me a mirror, he again prepared me, "You're going to get a shock, but don't be alarmed. The wounds are still very recent, and with time and care everything will be all right. You'll still look like you did on television."

My hand was shaking when I took the delicate mirror, finely framed with wrought bronze; this time, it was I who postponed the encounter with my image. I was frightened, I couldn't look, I feared the worst...

It was the worst.

When I saw the extent of the damage, I nearly fainted. It wasn't possible; it wasn't me... My whole body froze. I mustn't shout, I mustn't cry. Above all, I mustn't cry. I made a superhuman effort to hold back the tears, for fear my mother would also burst into sobs. I saw her biting her lip. I had to hold myself back. I had the sudden desire to vomit.

The mirror was shaking in my hands as I stared with awful fascination at that unrecognizable image of myself. My face was nothing more than a mass of formless, swollen flesh, striped with scars and covered in purple bruises and scabs. My eyes were now no more than two tiny holes lost in that battered, hideous form. After a long, silent inspection, I put the mirror down next to me. A nurse took my hand and I squeezed it very hard. I mustn't cry... I implored my mother with my eyes: don't cry, Mummy, I beg you. Don't cry.

It took me several hours to get over the shock. It was obvious to me that my husband had deliberately gone for my face. I was certain that he had not wanted to kill me but to disfigure me—to make me ugly so that I would no longer be desirable and no longer attract men. He was jealous of everything. Of the men who saw me on television, with a veil covering only my head, not my face. Of his friends who—rarely—caught sight of my hair, in the privacy of our apartment; he had carefully selected them, but it made no difference. He didn't trust them. After they had gone, there were frequent incredible scenes in which Rachid accused me of a smile, a look, or a word—when I hadn't lifted my eyes or opened my mouth the whole evening. He became completely paranoid, to the point that I dreaded the rare moments when I might have relaxed a little in company. My husband even took offense at my mother and forbade me to see her more than once a week.

But his chronic jealousy didn't stop there. It went much further and deeper: Rachid was jealous of my success and of the celebrity that had escaped him. His singing career had come to an end and he had not got over this failure. Convinced of his talent, he couldn't accept that he had been relegated to the wings; such was his pride that he saw this as an injustice. And, to cap it all off, I was a star! It was I who appeared on television, who was invited to dinner—even if I usually had to refuse these invitations because of my husband—and who was feted and applauded. Rachid could not bear it. By destroying my face, he would ensure that my television career and my celebrity were over. I would not overshadow him any more. I was convinced that that had been his goal—a goal he had achieved.

A heavy silence fell over the room. No one dared look me in the face; everyone looked at me out of the corner of their eyes, watching my reactions. Only the nurse stared, like me, at my image in the mirror.

The doctor was the first to speak.

"Rania, you will need to be patient, as I said to you, and brave. The marks will fade and I promise you that we will put your face back together. You must trust us."

"Yes, doctor. Thank you, doctor. Everything will be all right."

I spoke the words mechanically. They echoed in my head, wounding me: "Yes, doctor. Thank you, doctor." I just wanted him to leave; I didn't want to hear him any more. My vision began to dance; my face in the mirror became blurred, silhouettes around me began to shake and become malformed. Everything was giving way. Someone spoke to me but I didn't understand much of what they said. I caught only: "She is tired and we should let her rest. She needs to sleep."

One by one, my parents and friends left the room. I saw my mother waving her hand and then the door closed gently. I was finally alone. Slowly, I picked the mirror up again. It was terrible. I looked like no human being on earth. I couldn't recognize myself. I couldn't believe it—I didn't exist any more. I was looking at someone else. It couldn't be true... I had been a woman, a pretty woman, but now I was a monster. Where was the face that I had enjoyed seeing every morning in my bathroom mirror? I wasn't ashamed of having done that; God had blessed me with attractive features and I was thankful and appreciative. I liked being attractive because I felt I was spreading happiness around me. It wasn't narcissism but simply a sense of well-being and of gratitude.

I couldn't take my eyes off the disaster. Of the sweet face that had been mine, there remained only ruins and abandoned, ravaged ground. I didn't believe the doctor: I would never get my face back. I was going to be someone else. My whole life had crumbled. I would have to learn to be ugly. Ugly? I didn't know what that was! How did that feel? How would people look at me? Indeed, *would* people look at me? Beauty was certainly not everything, and women without it had many other assets and pleasures, but to have it and then lose it was something else entirely. To have been beautiful but to be no longer… Suddenly I realized that Rachid's plan had worked perfectly. It was Machiavellian in its ingenuity: not only would I return, like him, to anonymity, but I sensed that I too would find it hard to bear. I had gotten used to a life of glamour and fame. My husband's attack was also a theft; he had forced me into his shadows and condemned me to share his disappointment. The wounds covering my face were cruel evidence of this.

Over the following days, my mother and my sisters Raham and Rahab took turns sleeping beside me. My mother would gaze at me for a long time, thanking God for having let me live, even if I were deformed and mutilated. For my part, I wondered if I wouldn't rather have died. I began to appreciate the requirement for Muslim women to wear the veil. At least I could hide my face without anyone questioning why. That was something. The doctors came to examine me regularly. Bit by bit they began to tell me about a whole series of operations, first to remove the pockets of blood and then to reduce the multiple fractures. Exactly how many fractures were there? Difficult to count. In certain places, the bones of the face were so fragile that they had shattered into several little pieces, which they would have to try to put back together. I began to realize the enormity of the task and the time that would be needed for me to become presentable again, if I would one day become so. In any case,

I was soon certain that I would never look like I had before. I would have a new face, a new being, and new feelings. A stranger... The doctors didn't dare deny it; they only reassured me that the result would be satisfactory. I felt I was losing my identity.

Nonetheless, I forgave my husband and I wanted him to know it. But I also wanted to tell him clearly that there was no question of living together again, however much he repented. If he did repent. I forgave him in the name of the couple we once were, and above all in the name of our children. I didn't want to impose their father's banishment on them and I also encouraged them to forgive so that they would be at peace. As for Rachid, I knew, as a believer, that he would not escape God's punishment, either here or in another life.

In order to convey these messages, I needed more than ever to see journalists. Although my father never came to see me again, I knew he had no objection to this. On the contrary. He too wanted me to express myself and wanted my photo to be published—but for other reasons. He wanted revenge and for the whole country to know what my husband had done. He demanded justice. Our approaches were very different, but for the moment we both wanted to express ourselves in public and that was the important thing.

With my father's authorization, the first reporter soon came to my room, accompanied by a photographer: the representatives of a Saudi daily paper printed in Arabic and English. They didn't dare comment on my appearance, but I could see they were horrified by my smashed, stitched-up face in all its deformity. The photographer asked me half-heartedly for permission to take photos, obviously thinking I would refuse. He was truly surprised when I accepted and my father also agreed.

During the afternoon, a procession of journalists came to my bedside. A team from the channel where I worked came to take the first film footage. Again, I felt my friends were very embarrassed; I knew they had cried outside my room. They all cared for me very much and knew that my television career was over. My face was nothing but a field of beets, and they didn't know what angle to shoot it from. Of course, they too told me the doctors were confident and that it was only a matter of time, that I should not despair and that everyone was waiting for my return to the studio. They were all very kind and I thanked them for what they said, but no one was fooled.

I had a veritable stream of visitors. I began to realize the unexpected impact of my plight. I was not, unfortunately, the first woman in the country to have been beaten, but I was the first whose beating had unleashed such a storm. The fact that all the newspapers were rushing to talk about the attack and to condemn it astonished me. This was unheard of! Generally, few cases of the mistreatment of women are publicized, and over the course of the interviews I wondered whether I was a martyr or, despite myself, a militant.

I had agreed to give myself to the press so that we could discuss the problems in our society and how to resolve them ourselves. As a television newscaster who asked women to tell their stories, how could I refuse to do the same? I began to realize that talking was much more difficult than listening. I also realized that my society wanted to change, but didn't know how to do it. How could we just admit overnight that we treat women badly? That was a difficult boundary to cross. It was important first to arouse public interest in the problem in order to find solutions.

The next day, my horrific portrait was spread across the front page of all the newspapers, and MBC-FM broadcast an interview with me. It was a very difficult time for me. I imagined the comments: "And she was so pretty..." Yes— and she isn't any more! Far from it. It was no longer only my mirror that showed me the terrible image of what was left of my face, but the television screen and the front page of all the dailies. I was no longer enduring my crisis alone in the privacy of my room, but in front of everyone. The whole world could see my permanently destroyed face. Would they at least understand the fate that sometimes befalls women?

Here was the problem: to undertake serious reforms in Saudi Arabia was to attack a deeply rooted male culture in which women had little place outside the kitchen and the bedroom. But additionally, those who make the decisions in Saudi Arabia uniformly belong to the wealthy classes, whose women in many ways have more freedoms. The ruling class tends to be deaf to the demands and problems of the rest of the country, and especially to the plight of the average Saudi woman.

That was why I came at the right time, with my black eyes and my shattered face. I came at the right time because I was known and popular. The country had gotten used to seeing my face on television. I was no longer just a woman but part of daily life; I was a familiar image that had been destroyed. In mutilating me, my husband had also deprived the people of a familiar image, and that was serious.

So serious that the emir of Jeddah had told one of his close circle (who reported it to me) that he violently condemned Rachid's action, declaring that the police would do everything necessary to find him and that he would be severely punished, as the law required. The emir also wished me a speedy recovery and hoped that the experience would soon be no more than a painful memory for me.

When I heard this, I was so moved that I got goose-bumps. Another great first! For an emir, a member of the royal family, to come to the aid of an abused woman and castigate her attacker was unprecedented. It was even unthinkable. Perhaps, at that time of international crisis, when Saudi Arabia was being pinpointed and suspected of secretly encouraging terrorism, the emir wanted to show that Saudi society was evolving. The fact that he took such a position, even privately, marked a turning point. I had no doubt that his sentiments would be amplified and that we would see a desire for change. It was encouraging.

I completely understood the overriding importance of this declaration and was aware of the consequences. I thought of my husband, who would now feel hunted from all sides, if he had not committed suicide, as I still feared. I imagined that he was overwhelmed by the media attention. He had dreamed of celebrity and now he had it. But he would certainly rather not have this kind of fame.

The announcement of the emir's support quickly made the rounds at the hospital. I was already being pampered; now I was treated like a queen. My pillows were continually propped up, I was cosseted, stuffed with food, and my every little pain was tended. And this was only the beginning.

One morning, I heard a sudden commotion around me and in the corridors. People were running around, talking loudly, calling out; officers had filled the corridors and I heard orders being given. I had no idea what was going on. Soon after, nurses ran into my room to spruce me up while a battalion of cleaning women polished my room, which was in any case always impeccable. I tried to calm everyone down: "What's going on? Why are you so busy?"

"You don't know? The palace telephoned—Princess Sarah is coming."

How could I have known? I was stuck in my bed, still much too weak to get up alone, and I avoided using my cell phone because my multiple fractures made it extremely difficult to speak clearly.

Several minutes later, while a nurse was inspecting my room one last time, there was a knock on the door. Sarah appeared. The nurse disappeared with a curtsy.

Sarah! Princess Sarah, the wife of the emir of Jeddah, had taken the trouble to come and visit me. I was very honored. She is an extraordinary woman whom I'd known for a short time; we had met at a reception and had immediately hit it off. The princess is the founder of a charitable association that she runs energetically, giving herself entirely to its large-scale social projects. She is particularly concerned with ensuring that poor children have enough to eat and access to medical care. She is also concerned with abused women—coincidentally—and the Egyptian government had given her an award for all her activities.

The first time we met, Princess Sarah had asked me to join her association. I had happily accepted. Several days later we had gone together to the north of the country, to the Bedouin village that Sarah was helping settle in one place. Thanks to her moral and financial support, not only were they building houses that were gradually replacing their ancestral tents, but they had been able to bring water and electricity to their village—the height of luxury for these people. It was hardly surprising that the princess had been received with the greatest honor and deference in these places, although that was not why she had gone there. When we arrived, no sooner had she gotten out of the car than I saw her talking to a group of women, asking about their health and the children who were clinging to their skirts. Then she talked to the head of the village to find out how the work was advancing and ensure that the water conveyance was working properly. I had been impressed by her dynamism and her simplicity.

That same simplicity of attitude was there with me in my hospital room. Sarah was cheerful and smiling. Far from lamenting my fate, she encouraged me to take on my situation and fight it. She didn't go over what had happened, which she knew to be pointless, but turned to the future and considered ways to fight against such attacks and to help me recover from the one that had nearly killed me. The princess did not content herself with outlining the courses of action but offered solutions. She announced she was going to launch a powerful support campaign for me. "We should fight to stop violence against women. I am going to mobilize all the women in my association to support you."

I immediately realized the impact of such a movement. The members of the association were all members of the aristocracy and their influence was immense, as was that of their husbands—who were for the most part open to progressive ideas even if they could not, for political and cultural reasons, always express this. The country was not ready for a radical transformation, especially not at the urging of other nations. Reform, however necessary, had to come from within. The people would not tolerate foreigners dictating their choices; fundamentalists would be the primary beneficiaries of such a mistaken policy, as the men in power knew only too well.

For once, the opportunity was ripe. I didn't choose it and would willingly, truth be told, have passed it by, but I was an ideal figurehead for a campaign: I was Saudi, I was a completely innocent victim, and I enjoyed considerable popularity. It was the moment to take advantage of all that, as Sarah explained to me, with her habitual enthusiasm. She was almost to the point of thanking me for the helping hand that I had lent her cause...

Her battle plan laid out, she declared that she would take on all my medical and hospital bills. She had already contacted leading surgeons and they had assured her that they would be able to give a human form back to my face, although it would involve several serious operations.

This visit from Princess Sarah did me enormous good. When she left my room with a last wave of the hand, I made the effort to get up by myself and walked to the window to watch her cross the hospital courtyard.

The following day, all the newspapers talked about the visit. The Rania al-Baz affair had gained new force and taken on a new dimension; now it symbolized the emancipation of women. By coming to my bedside, the wife of the emir of Jeddah, one of the most important people in the country, had pledged her support to that cause. It was a real revolution that gave me courage.

Over the next hours, representatives of the foreign press also streamed to my bedside. As I had predicted, the princess's visit caused a great stir. I received journalists from all over the world—Agence France-Presse, the largest British agencies, the Associated Press, and Reuters. This was clearly no longer a simple local news story. It was nothing less than a catalyst for major and explosive reform.

Two days later, I underwent my first cosmetic surgery. The surgeons first treated the pockets of blood that deformed my face and prevented them from dealing with the fractures. How long did the operation last? I have no idea, but when I awoke, a doctor ran to my bedside. He seemed worried.

"How do you feel, Rania?"

I didn't feel that badly, although I had a furred tongue and my head was heavy. I stammered several reassuring words, although I could see that something was wrong and that the surgeon was ill at ease. Cautiously, he warned me: "We had some problems. We had to stop the operation and we have to start again. Be brave and relax. We're going to give you some tranquilizers."

Still knocked out by the anesthetic, I didn't take in what he was telling me. It was only the following day, when my bandages were undone, that I was shell-shocked. Nothing had changed. If anything, my face was worse. I was desperate, convinced that I would look like a monster for the rest of my life. I didn't believe in doctors anymore. I didn't believe in anything anymore; I was done for.

A second operation was planned for a few days later. I resigned myself to it. In my condition, I didn't have much to lose.

This time, the operation was a success. My face was cleared of bumps and hematomas. It was a first, satisfactory step, but the deformity of my nose was now emphasized: a horrific lump that was immediately noticeable. I waited impatiently for the surgeon to give it back some shape. I didn't dare look at myself. I put off the moment of truth and in the meantime gave everything over to God. After having listened to my chest, the doctor plunged me a little further into my despair. His verdict was terrible: "I can do nothing. It's inoperable."

It was too hard a blow. I couldn't live with this horror— it was impossible. I begged the doctor but it did no good; he refused. My kind Princess Sarah immediately began looking for another practitioner, but several refused before one, Mazen Fteani, accepted the risk, although he warned me that he could not guarantee the result and that I would have to wait six months before my nose took on its definitive shape.

To give me back a presentable face, three other operations followed the one on my nose. The doctors were meticulous, having to put back together the bones that had been broken in several pieces. They worked miracles, but despite their skill I still couldn't recognize myself, which shook me psychologically. Throughout the whole period of my operations I constantly looked at myself in the mirror to follow the development of my scars and above all my nose—not so much because of narcissism as for a search for my identity. I was consumed with anxiety and haunted by my past.

Preoccupied by this quest and tired from all the operations, I didn't realize that my story continued to go around the world, inciting emotion and polemic, until the day when I learned that thousands of miles from Jeddah, in Washington, DC, an American politician had quoted my case as an example during a debate on foreign policy to prove that the Middle East was changing.

Reports echoed back to me from all over the world: from Paris, London, Berlin, Tokyo, and Buenos Aires, our ambassadors called to tell of newspaper articles and TV programs that covered my story, sometimes accompanied by extreme remarks. The condition of Saudi Arabian women was often presented in rather simplistic and absolute terms. Women were depicted as slaves, without it being pointed out that we are also devoted to our religion, culture, and traditions; it wasn't that everything imposed on us, or that we imposed on ourselves, was negative. It was only excesses and abuses that should be denounced. My case was the model example of this.

But the great international women's organizations reacted more sympathetically, and while I was convalescing and the surgeons were improving on their work with small, finishing touches, I received a huge postbag of letters of support and encouragement from all over the world, along with offers to join feminist movements or invitations to take part in conferences.

One e-mail came from France, from a movement that I of course did not know but which bore a name so strange and shocking that it immediately attracted my attention: *Ni putes, ni soumises* [Neither prostitute, nor submissive]. My first reaction was revulsion. Then I reflected more by analyzing the provocative aspect of the words. Neither prostitute nor submissive?

Not a prostitute? Were Saudis concerned by this? I really didn't think so. Given the strictness of our Qur'anic laws and of our culture, I found it hard to imagine that a woman would run the risk of prostitution. Even the word was taboo. That said, I had nonetheless heard about prostitutes in Saudi Arabia and so, in my work as a journalist, I had decided to investigate. I ultimately discovered four prostitutes, who I spoke to about their lives. At first they denied they were prostitutes, but in the end admitted that unemployment and poverty had forced them to sell themselves. Our society didn't offer any other escape route for them. They had been desperate.

So I asked myself: what did these French women mean by "prostitute"? It soon seemed to me that they wanted to clarify the term and its function. A prostitute is a woman who sells her body, not, in a usage I'd heard in my country, a woman who uses her body as she (and not her father or husband) wishes. The former is different from the latter. But who is responsible? Who is guilty? Who is the prostitute— the woman who sells herself or the man who encourages her to do so? A hungry stomach doesn't have a conscience. These women need to live and have nothing to sell but their bodies. Allah condemns prostitution, but we shouldn't accuse those who brave the injunction, only those who force them to do so to earn their money. Let us go even further: oil for food was the deal offered to Iraq. Was that not prostitution? And the journalist who sells himself for money or fame? That is real prostitution! Whoever sells his conscience prostitutes himself.

And not submissive? That was easier to understand. Women should not submit to any arbitrary authority, including that of men. In the name of what? I was in a good position to know the cost, in Saudi Arabia, of infringing upon the widespread male domination.

And so, yes, neither prostitute nor submissive were the conditions I desired for my peers, and it was within that framework that I wanted to see women grow and affirm ourselves. It was because I had refused to submit that Rachid had wanted to destroy me. I was no longer his possession or his object; he was no longer the dominant male and he could neither tolerate nor accept that. Can we accept such male chauvinism at the beginning of the 21st century? No.

And so I read carefully the text that accompanied an invitation to take part in a conference in Paris of *Ni putes, ni soumises*. In a few lines, the movement presented itself and set out its aims: to struggle for the recognition of women's rights and for their dignity. In the state I was in, I thought it was high time to concern myself with these aims and I had a sudden desire to fight. I just wanted to know a little more about the French movement before I agreed to take part in the conference.

The vice president, Mohammed Abdi, explained to me over the phone that the association had been created to speak out against the condition of young Muslim women in certain troubled areas of the big French cities with large North African and African populations. At first the group had formed spontaneously, but their idea was innovative and courageous, and the public had been so supportive that the founders of the movement were able to structure it and give it a legal framework. Today the organization has an office in the twelfth arrondissement of Paris and comprises more than 6,000 members in France, both men and women, with branches in several countries, including Morocco, Tunisia, and Algeria, which represented a real advance and required a good deal of courage on the part of those who ran the centers.

And that was why, having got these details, I too forged ahead: yes to the conference, planned for October 2004.

Mohammed was delighted to learn of my decision. He told me of the difficulty he'd had, with his friends Asma, Siham, and Fadela, in tracking me down. The idea of inviting me had come to them when they read an article about me in a British magazine in April. The photo of my swollen face had horrified them and they thought that my testimony could become one of the central features of their fall conference. To invite me they had had to find me first, which wasn't so easy. With the help of journalists from the British magazine they had managed to get my e-mail address and had written to me. They later told me that they had not really believed they would get a favorable response. Mohammed Abdi even made me laugh by telling me that he had thought I would refuse to speak to him, believing that it was forbidden for a Saudi woman to speak to a man. The Qur'an does not prohibit it, except if the woman provokes the man sexually. Indeed, it was Aisha, the Prophet's wife, who gave her husband's teachings to his disciples.

I therefore agreed and was even happy to do so because I needed to speak, to externalize my experience, and to talk to the world in order to try to stop these practices. Some people saw my decision as courageous. Perhaps. For myself, I saw it above all as a cry for help and a desire for protection. By putting myself in the spotlight, I hoped to discourage those who still might secretly want to harm me but who would be too cowardly to do so in public. By exposing myself to everyone's gaze, I hoped to become untouchable. The more I could make my voice heard, the less easily I could be silenced. It was obvious that the media uproar over my case was not to everyone's liking—but luckily I had the support of the Saudi authorities. I knew that even if they could not say so publicly, many decision makers secretly encouraged me to testify. By denouncing the condition of women in our country, I would give them the weapons they lacked and arguments they could present against those who wanted to refuse all change.

Knowing that I had official support reassured me in my precisely targeted struggle. For, to be clear, I respect both Saudi Arabia and Islam and I didn't want it to be thought that I was fighting either one. The Qur'an does not, and the laws of our country do not, authorize a man to beat his wife. That was what I wanted to clarify and nothing more. I do not condemn our traditions, our culture, or our rules; I oppose only those who have abused them and who have created their own code in the name of Allah. This was what I wanted to do in Paris. I was impatient to be there.

The thought of the trip to France lifted my spirits, but the prospect of showing myself in public brought me brutally back to reality: was I presentable? After the operation on my nose, I had undergone three smaller cosmetic surgeries, which had nonetheless left scars. The surgeons had assured me that they would fade, but for now they were still there.

I went into my bathroom to see if my face was presentable in public or if I should give up on the idea. The aftereffects of the operations were clearly visible, but there were still many weeks to go before October. I could hope for a real improvement by then. My nose, which had posed so many problems, was healing well. It now had a more or less normal shape. I hardly had the fine and delicate features of which I had been proud, but I was learning to be satisfied with my new face. It was very hard to accept but I had no choice. Judging that I would be presentable by October, I put on some make-up—for the first time since my operations—and saw that creams and foundations disguised the damage very well. That would do! Especially as those who would attend the event knew what had happened to me; I wasn't going to a fashion show.

Indeed, the whole world knew what had happened to me, and I was in demand from all sides when, at the end of June, my husband gave himself up to the police. The police alerted me immediately. For me, it was an immense relief. He was alive. I confirmed to both the police and the judges that I forgave him; my position on that had not altered. I was thinking above all of the children. I wanted them to grow up in peace. Justice had to take its course, however, and Rachid would have to be tried. My pardon would be taken into account and might lessen the sentence—but for the moment the process of the trial did not concern me. The judges would decide.

This new development did nothing to lessen my determination. I forgave in my own name but I would fight in the name of women.

In October, I went to Paris. I was very pleased to be once more in a city I liked and where I had already spent several days with my husband on our honeymoon. Mohammed Abdi and Asma, another leader of *Ni putes, ni soumises*, were waiting for me at Roissy airport and accompanied me to the plush Sofitel Saint-Jacques hotel, where all the delegates were staying. We hit it off immediately and Asma and I were already chatting like two old friends when we walked into the lobby of the hotel. She would become my most faithful and sincere Parisian friend; we would talk at length and our friendship allowed us to overcome all our points of disagreement.

I kissed her goodbye as if it were the most natural thing in the world when she left me to relax for a few hours before the conference's opening dinner. It would be an opportunity to meet, exchange ideas, and get a good sense of everyone's contribution.

The fall conference of *Ni putes, ni soumises* would take place over three days. I would speak twice, on Friday and Sunday. Though it was my first conference, I wasn't that nervous. My job in television meant that I was familiar with the microphone and I had often had to speak in public during live broadcasts. I was used to this kind of situation. What worried me more was the content of my speech and the message I wanted to convey. I had to be very clear so that what I said was well understood and my words could not be misinterpreted. After dinner, I reread the speech I had prepared, weighing for the last time the words I had so carefully chosen.

The following day, we left the capital and went to Dourdan, a district in the western suburbs where the conference would be held. A holiday association, Village Vacances Famille, had given the movement a room to use. A large banner was stretched across the outside of the building: "The fight for women's liberation: an international and democratic campaign."

Since I had traveled so far from my home, I was in a good position to see the necessity of an international campaign to address the suffering of women. An isolated country cannot itself adequately confront poverty and injustice. In order to progress, countries must unite their efforts and share their knowledge and technology. And in the future, countries will have to unite further to distribute the fruits of this progress equally among all. All oppressed women should group together to act to mobilize democracies. It is the only way to move forward. This was what I was going to say.

Six hundred people were attending the conference. The participants were quite young but every social class seemed to be represented. Although there were more women than men, skin color was equally balanced among white, black, and brown. The atmosphere was good-natured and relaxed, though everyone listened with great seriousness.

When my turn came, I immediately highlighted the issue that seemed the most important in my story: "I wasn't beaten in the name of a religious principle but by a jealous and angry man—that is all. Those who take refuge behind Islam to justify such actions are lying and those who sincerely believe—as some do—that the Qur'an encourages these practices are mistaken. They are manmade practices, nothing more. The Prophet teaches love, not the hate that certain of his zealots are propagating today."

The more I spoke, the more impassioned I became; I didn't realize that the audience was also becoming impassioned. I lived my speech intensely, passing from emotion to laughter, and soon the hall burst into applause.

After having recounted my story, as I had been asked, I drew the inevitable conclusions: now I had to fight, not just for myself but for all women who suffered and who didn't have the means to defend themselves. I finished my talk with this warning: "Let us never forget that in some parts of the world those men and women who join our struggle will die. We should fight for them."

Applause thundered around me. It was a great moment. I understood then that I had committed myself to a major cause that I would have to defend with all my strength. I knew, alas, that the road would be long.

At the end of the first day of the conference, Fadela introduced me to a tall, distinguished man with white hair, who honored me by kissing my hand in what seemed to me a manner of great political protocol. I wasn't wrong, for it was Dominique de Villepin, then the French foreign minister. We exchanged a few words in English against the flash of photographs and television cameras. The minister congratulated me on my courage and determination.

The following day, pictures of our interview were all over the papers, including in Muslim countries, which gave me great pleasure. My photo was again going around the world, this time not as a battered, humiliated woman, but a free woman who was fighting for her cause.

Before leaving France, I took advantage of this celebrity to transmit my message to the wider public. I was first invited onto the 8 o'clock news on the TV channel France 2 and then onto a popular current affairs program. Each time I repeated my call for help and mobilization. Speaking out in public was absolutely necessary to raise public consciousness.

My engagement was such that my friends from *Ni putes, ni soumises* feared for my security upon my return to Saudi Arabia. They insisted that I alert them immediately if I felt threatened or anxious.

But I wasn't worried; I knew I had the government's support. What is more, on my arrival back in Jeddah, I received a private call from a high government dignitary whom I didn't know. What he said totally reassured me.

"Hello, Rania, you were charming. The Europeans got to see an educated, strong, beautiful Saudi woman, in stark contradiction to the images of our country that are usually peddled around—desert, camels, and illiterate women."

It was true that the journalists whom I had met had not expected such discourse. They told me that I had become the "princess of Paris." There was no need to exaggerate!

Shortly after my return to Jeddah, the women's magazine *Saiditi*, the Saudi *Elle*, devoted a long article to me and outlined my activities in France. In the interview, I nonetheless slightly changed the name of the organization that had invited me. "Neither prostitute nor submissive" would not have gone over well in Saudi Arabia. We couldn't rush things.

After such a media exposure, I needed to catch my breath and reflect. Feeling more relaxed, I took stock of all that had happened. How had I gotten to this point, and why?

A Submissive Woman

T he perfectly straight roads of Riyadh, the Saudi capital, or of Jeddah, the great Red Sea port that looks toward Mecca, are filled with gleaming American cars that regularly stop in front of little ancient stalls run by bearded men with faces as dried up and crumpled as withered grapes. At the gates of the cities, powerful 4x4s head into the desert along rectilinear roads, which are continually cleared of sand, to several tents planted in the middle of a herd of camels. The future and the past coexist, obstinately refusing to separate.

Born in the 1970s, I am a member of the computer generation. Yet when I was a child, we still had slaves in my home. One of them—discreetly rechristened an "employee" when King Faisal abolished slavery after his ascension to the throne in 1964—was even destined for my use. I was eventually to have received him as a gift from my grandmother, according to the tradition of wealthy families, until I brutally damaged one of his eyes while playing with him too roughly when I was two, pushing a glass into his face. In compensation, my embarrassed family offered him a small shop. He still spends his time there happily and is almost grateful to me.

This exploitation of human beings may seem shocking, but you have to understand that my grandparents still belonged to another age. They could have emerged straight out of a story from the *Thousand and One Nights*. Not adapting very well to the modern age, they fiercely bemoaned the loss of the way of life they had known growing up. The story of their meeting and marriage would today be inconceivable—and yet it took place as recently as the 1930s. Time has raced ahead since then.

The first surprise in their story is that my paternal grandfather was blond, with long, light hair falling to his shoulders, an inheritance from his Turkish origins. His family was brought to Mecca by the Ottoman waves that entered the country after the 16th century. We do not know exactly when his ancestors arrived in the region; probably toward the end of the 19th century, according to the memory handed down through the generations.

At that time, the borders of present-day Saudi Arabia had not yet been defined. Oil would not be discovered there until 1938. When my family settled in Mecca, majestic caravans transporting textiles, salt, and spices wove their way across the desert. They made their fortune in trade. My grandfather was rich and lived with his family in a three-story stone building, which he owned. Among other businesses, he had a bookshop near the Ka'aba that sold mainly sacred texts.

This privileged situation allowed him to have the prettiest women and, from the stories I have heard, he indulged himself, not sparing his riches to procure the ones he liked.

Slavery was at that time legal and traditional and no one thought of denouncing it. Today, such practices offend our consciences, but at the time people of my grandparents' class found nothing wrong with it. Traffickers had set up slave networks in Yemen, Africa, and Asia and would go there to seize whole contingents of men and women destined for labor and harems. Strong young men and pretty young women were the most sought after. Bands of strictly organized thugs didn't hesitate to attack whole villages, even in remote regions of Saudi Arabia, to take youngsters and sell them in the big cities.

And so it was that one day one of these desert pirates offered an exceptionally beautiful young girl, Farah, to my grandfather; he bought her immediately, not worrying where she had come from, and was so impressed with her beauty that he married her. Farah was just thirteen. Some months later she gave birth to a bouncing boy who would become my uncle Hassan. To be such a young mother was nothing extraordinary in Saudi Arabia. As soon as girls entered puberty, they were considered women and marriageable—and therefore able to give birth.

My grandfather rejoiced in the son that Farah had given him. Lost in his happiness, he didn't ask any questions. Little did he imagine that 400 kilometers away, in the south of the country, the young girl's disappearance had not gone unnoticed; it had even caused a small revolution, and her father was ready to send an army to get her back if necessary. For he was also very attached to the child and had gone into a rage when he had discovered that she had been taken. For him it was not just a violent separation, but a serious offense to be avenged.

Had the kidnappers made a mistake or had they known what they were doing? Either way, their action caused a great stir in Farah's village, which was extremely unusual. Generally, slave traders stole children and adolescents from very humble backgrounds. When their families discovered the loss, that was the end of the story: kidnapping was a fatality, a fact of life no less than a child dying of illness. Complain? To whom? The country had little formal structure and the poorest had to submit to the law of the more powerful.

Farah's father was not poor, however. He was very wealthy and not in the habit of letting himself be dispossessed without responding. He too knew the law of the sword and was not afraid of it. As soon as he knew that his daughter had been taken, he launched an army of spies to find her. Dozens of private detectives, in burnoose and babouches, mainly recruited from the same troubled milieu as the highway bandits who had stolen Farah in the first place, immediately began combing the country to find the child. Knowing the world of the traffickers well, they were the best placed to trace the ringleaders, but the camels were slow and the desert vast. Their search took some time.

However, bit by bit the information filtered through and the trail appeared. Having already impregnated his young wife, my grandfather had no idea that a noose was tightening around him and that he would soon have to account for a marriage to which he alone had consented.

Shortly after my uncle Hassan was born, the first emissary from Farah's father presented himself to my grandfather, after having formally identified my grandfather's young wife. Not being authorized to act, he contented himself with outlining the situation to my grandfather, warning that his bride's father was en route to Mecca and that he could expect some forceful discussion.

It is tempting to imagine that what came next was a row, blows, threats, insults, revenge, a demand for apologies, compensation—that would be logical.

But no! Nothing of the sort happened.

General de Gaulle once said, as he was setting off for a trip to our region, "I am flying with my simple notions to a complex East." It was a perceptive remark. If the East is not more complicated than the West, it *is* different, with different forms of reasoning, as worthy as Western logic as they are unlike it.

Since the harm had already been done, rather than killing each other and launching into an interminable vendetta, my paternal grandfather and my maternal great-grandfather chose instead to sit around a table and negotiate.

It was nonetheless a tense negotiation, by all accounts. It was not kidnapping that posed the problem—that was accepted—but the fact that it had happened to a rich family, who did not expect its daughters to be treated like slaves. Farah's father hoped for more for his daughter and was accustomed to making his own choices. He therefore saw the methods that had been used as a crime of *lèse-majesté* that demanded reparation. For the rest, they could come to some agreement.

"The rest" was Farah. It was as if the sky came tumbling down on her head when she was forced to decide between her father and her husband—neither of whom she had chosen.

For at the end of their dealings, the two men arrived at this resolution: Farah had indeed been taken by force, but she was now officially married—without the consent of her father, and that was the problem. This was inconceivable in the Muslim world and Islam had no provision for this kind of blunder: an abduction without intent to harm. For the kidnappers had not in fact wanted to harm—they had made a mistake whose consequences they could not have foreseen. There must be a solution. It was only a matter of finding it.

Well! Exceptionally, Farah was going to be allowed to decide whether to validate her marriage and so to choose her father or her husband—although "allowed" is overstating the case. In fact, she was urged to decide her fate by carefully weighing the consequences of her decision, as if she were the one who had committed a fault! The victim had been transformed into the guilty party.

Try to imagine such a situation today. What would happen if a child were taken at the age of thirteen, torn away from her family by armed ruffians and sold to a stranger who made her his wife and forced her into his bed? Simple: as soon as the plot had been discovered, the poor child would be handed over to an army of psychologists and her torturers would be thrown in prison.

Here, not only was no one concerned with the trauma suffered by the victim, but her father did not tear her away from the hands of these brutes while demanding justice: instead, he negotiated! For he laid out clearly to her that if she refused to go back with him, as he proposed, she would never be welcome in the family again and would cease to exist for them. Take it or leave it. Charming.

For his part, her husband warned her that if she left she would never see her child again and that she was hardly likely to find another man with such wealth or comforts to offer.

Revolting and offensive blackmail. One might imagine that this would have been another reason for the young mother to take refuge in her family, begging her father to do everything he could to get the child. But this was not France, Britain, or the United States. At fourteen, Farah knew that if she rejoined the paternal fold she would soon be married again—without her opinion being asked—like her grandmother, mother, sisters, and cousins before her. Did the prospect please her? Who knows? In any case, it didn't shock her. It was normal and had always been the lot of girls of marriageable age. Almost none of them knew that in other parts of the world things were very different. They accepted the custom, or at least resigned themselves to it.

Farah therefore carefully considered her options. Her husband was not wrong: she knew what she had, but not what she could expect in several months or even several weeks, because her father gave her no information. What is more, despite her youth Farah was probably attached, like all women, to her son. She must have been deeply distressed by the idea of not seeing him anymore. The two men imposed a cruel choice on her and demanded that she pronounce her decision in court so that it would be legally recorded. The young girl made her choice: she would stay with her husband. But for the judges to give her that right she had to renounce her father and declare that he was not her progenitor.

Farah therefore chose her present over an uncertain future. And there was no going back on that decision: what was done was done. For her father, Farah no longer existed.

Some time later, my grandfather married a second wife, who was from Yemen. She too took up residence in the family home. She would have three children: a girl and two boys, including my favorite uncle, Farid. But it was Farah, the first wife, who gave birth to my father, Yahia. He grew up in Mecca without the slightest shadow of any worry. He had a happy and problem-free childhood, under the protection of his parents and his big brother, Uncle Farid.

This uncle was a lovable character. He was the center of the family, acting as both its driving force and its unifier, watching over everyone and ensuring their welfare. My father lived peacefully under his rule until he was old enough to marry.

As a student, my father was very attractive to women. He was the Don Juan of the area and everyone knew his repu-tation. One day, one of my uncles, Anwar, who was more timid than my father, told him that he had seen a fantastic girl in a neighboring building. My father immediately went on the prowl. He wanted to judge for himself, and climbed up to the roof of our house to see this jewel. After hours of wait-ing, he glimpsed the object of his desire and it was love at first sight. She was indeed a real beauty. Father lost his head— he couldn't restrain himself. He wanted to meet her and even marry her straightaway. He therefore asked his father to request the girl's hand from her parents. He was twenty-one and the girl who would become my mother was fourteen.

The affair was swiftly concluded, for the two families thought it an excellent match. I have no complaints: I have a great admiration for my mother, who gave me and my seven brothers and sisters an excellent education and passed on to us her love of beauty.

My mother is a fashionable, bourgeois woman who loves luxury and makes no secret of it. Our apartment in Mecca was furnished with infinite taste. Mother was always looking for pretty pieces of furniture and the finest china. She adored having friends to the house and it was a point of honor for her to set the most elegant table and to decorate with attention to the smallest details. My father did not seem to realize what efforts she went to in satisfying her guests, nor his good fortune in having found such a remarkable mistress of the house. Because he was a man, all these efforts seemed to him normal. In any case, it cannot be said that family life was usually at the center of his concerns. His main preoccupation was his accounting studies, which were far from over, and his first business dealings alongside his father.

As a small child, I suffered a lot from this lack of attention, particularly because my mother was not a great one for giving physical affection either. It was inevitable: she was so young. At just fifteen, she was herself a child in need of affection. She loved me a lot, but I was her doll; she wasn't mature enough for the duties that had been laid on her.

I remember one night when I had been crying for a good while in my bed; it was my uncle Farid, who lived on the floor above, who went to wake my mother so that she would finally attend to me.

At the time, my devotion to my uncle and aunt, an adorable and fashionable woman, made me climb upstairs to the next floor as soon as I could to go to their apartment. Their way of life fulfilled my little girl's dreams.

I also sought out my grandmother Farah. What an exquisite woman! From her I learned to cook, to sew, to embroider, and even to pick out the best tea. She was a Muslim woman to the tips of her chador, totally supportive of her husband, living only through him and for him. Her capacity for devotion was incredible. Whenever she did the laundry, she would examine my grandfather's clothes one by one to check their cleanliness. If they weren't clean enough for her liking, if she detected the least imperfection or if the white was not dazzling enough, she would wash them again, and then throw herself into long and artistic ironing sessions.

She saw no submissiveness in her approach. She saw herself as neither a slave nor inferior to men; she saw her work as a personal investment that gave her value and accomplished a mission desired by God. In safeguarding her husband's well-being and the cleanliness of his possessions, my grandmother was testifying to a deep respect for him, and in respecting him, she respected herself. Her attitude was spontaneous and unforced.

I always listened to her carefully when she explained the principles that guided her. She spoke with so much gentleness and conviction that what she said seemed to me nothing but obvious. To my little girl's mind, it all seemed normal, and I promised myself that I would do as good a job for my kind husband as she did for hers. He would also have the whitest and best-pressed shirts in Mecca so that the whole town would know that his wife was the most devoted, the most attentive, and the most skilled with her hands.

To this end, I began helping my grandmother with her household tasks when I was very young, folding and putting away the laundry with great care before trotting into the kitchen with her. There I would jump up onto a chair so as to be on the same level as her while she kneaded dough or skewered kebabs. My hands holding the back of my chair, my eyes level with the work surface, I would follow every detail of her movements. She communicated her knowledge and love of cooking to me. When I became a woman myself, it was always with pleasure that I slipped on an apron and launched into concocting, thanks to her, the most complicated dishes.

Spending most of my time as a child with my grandmother and my uncle and aunt, I didn't feel any great emotion when my mother told me one day that my father was going to leave us to pursue his studies in the United States. He was already so little present, in my eyes, that the announcement of his absence hardly saddened me. He was going? Good. The important thing was that my mother, grandmother, uncle, and aunt were staying. As for the United States, I didn't know where it was. At the edge of the town, a little farther into the desert, or still farther? I took the news in and then returned to my games, little understanding why the news created so much emotion in my family.

On the day of my father's departure, the whole household gathered in our building to say goodbye and wish him great luck. I was impressed by the seriousness of their faces. Something important was happening, but I didn't understand what it was, so it seemed best not to make my presence known. This was made easier by the fact that my father ignored me. Not worrying for a moment about whether I was there, he didn't even smile at me when, like everyone else, I waved as he disappeared into the car that would take him to Jeddah airport.

This non-event already seemed very distant when, several weeks later, my mother told me that we—she, my brothers and sisters, and I—would soon leave to join our father in those United States that I still could not situate. I was now told that they were on the other side of the sea, which didn't help me much further but left me skeptical. As a result, I began seriously to ask myself questions.

While my father's departure had left me indifferent, now I was split between excitement and anxiety. Yes! Now it was I, Rania, who was involved—it was I who was going, and not only that but going in an airplane. That was something, it had to be said! As soon as I knew that, I looked up all the time, watching out for those little shining dots in the sky heading off toward the sun. I had never yet flown in an airplane and was impatient, although a little scared, to try it.

Since the announcement of our departure, the whole house had been in uproar. I had the impression that I was living out of a suitcase, with parcels and piles of laundry everywhere.

And then the great day came. We were leaving for Washington.

My father had settled there. He had stayed first in a hotel, allowing him to adapt to the life of the country and to look for an apartment for him and his family. Saudi friends had helped him and it had not taken him long to find the furnished house to which we were now flying. What an adventure!

How beautiful it was, the airplane. The blue seats were much too big for me and I stretched my arms and legs out to fill the space. Mother was seated next to me, comfortably installed. Shortly after take-off she took off her veil, which she folded and put away in her bag. There weren't many women in the airplane but they almost all did the same thing and no one said anything to them. It must be permitted to take off one's veil in an airplane, as it was in the house. I would ask Mother later, but for the moment I preferred to glue my face against the window and look at the houses that were getting smaller and the desert that was getting bigger.

I slept for most of the journey and was still sleepy when we arrived in Washington. We waited for a long time, a very long time, while the police carefully checked Mother's passport. They finally let us go and I soon saw my mother with a small group of people behind a barrier. That woke me up. Then something incredible and completely unexpected happened: my father went up to my mother, smiled at her, took hold of her neck and… kissed her on the mouth! Yes, on the mouth, in front of everybody! I was flabbergasted. My eyes opened wide; I was certain that there would be an uproar, and that someone would come and hit my father, tear him away from my mother. I even hoped that my mother would defend herself or flee. Frightened, I looked around anxiously. Nothing moved. No one reacted and no one took any notice of my parents, as though nothing had happened. Father was still smiling and now mother also… Bizarre. America was beginning well.

This unexpected scene marked me for life. It shocked me deeply. I had never seen a man and a woman kiss. And on the lips! And it was my parents who had done it! My mind was in a complete whirlwind. I saw the act as a form of aggression, a violent and monstrous gesture that was unworthy of a man. My father had discredited himself and at that moment I hated him. I still think about it today and I forbid men from making the slightest inappropriate or familiar gesture in public, even when I am outside Saudi Arabia. It is a question of principle and correctness. Even my husband paid the price for this modesty.

Many years later, when I was walking with him in the streets of Paris, I again saw people kissing. Laughing, I said to my husband: "They're right; why kiss only in bed? I'd like to try it too." I was joking, but he took me seriously. A few minutes later, he tried to kiss me on an escalator in a shopping center. Horrors! I was filled with intense fear; I suddenly felt naked in front of everybody. I trembled all over and Rachid, who understood nothing, stammered, "But why ask for something you don't want?"

The house my father had rented was situated in a quiet residential area of Washington, DC, far from the center of the city. It was spacious, light, and comfortable, surrounded by a garden that contained a slide and green and red swings. It was all very pleasant, but I felt lost in the strange environment. It would take me several weeks to find my bearings and adapt to my new life. It wasn't easy. I went every day to a private school for Arabs, where I learned English. The other pupils were mainly the children of diplomats and businessmen from the Gulf states, and they behaved nothing like my friends in Mecca. For a while it bothered me somewhat, but my disturbance was nothing compared to my mother's.

My mother didn't take at all to her new existence and time did nothing to improve things. On the contrary, the more days that passed, the more my mother missed Saudi Arabia. It has to be said that my father's choice of this out-of-the-way part of Washington was incomprehensible. The Saudi community was grouped together in another part of the American capital and my mother couldn't understand why my father hadn't chosen a house near them. She would have felt less alone, could have met Arab friends with whom to go out and shop. Here she was isolated throughout the day in our villa in the middle of an elegant but unfriendly district populated by American executives whose private lives seemed to consist of jogging and TV dinners. For people who were used to activity after sunset, it was hardly ideal.

My mother could not understand what had motivated my father; living amid Saudis would have been much more pleasant even for him. It seemed a mystery.

In fact, his reasoning was simple. My father was terribly jealous and because my mother was a beautiful woman, he did not want to expose her to other men in the Saudi community who, far from their country, were bored and poorly integrated into American society. As cautious as a warlord who locked his beauty in the dungeon before leaving for battle, my father had chosen to isolate my mother so as to avoid all temptation.

The result was that my mother moped for days on end in front of a stultifying television, not daring to complain. It was very hard for a woman of the world to bear such a cloistered existence. She missed terribly the big receptions that she had organized and animated at our home in Mecca. She suggested to my father that she should organize some here, at least to meet people and to have a little fun, but the response was always a resounding refusal. My father would hear nothing of it. For him it was clear: if his friends met my mother, they wouldn't hesitate to travel the distance to see her again. This was what he believed and my mother had to put up with this unshakeable notion.

Our life rapidly became more and more sad. When he got back from the university where he was studying, my father barely spoke and showed no interest in us. He didn't think to find out how we were, or even less how we had spent our days. I found this lack of interest distressing and immensely frustrating. I often felt like crying—just like my mother. I would regularly see her in tears, wandering from one room to the other, with nothing to do and above all no desire to do anything. The woman who had been so active now spent hours hanging around to pass the time. I didn't recognize her anymore. Even sewing, which she had adored, gave her no pleasure. In Mecca she had often launched into creating fabulous wedding dresses, just for the fun of it, that were so fine and delicate that I would clap my hands in delight at the sight of them. Here, she had no enthusiasm for such things; her heart just wasn't in it. When I got back from school I would see that the work she had begun several days earlier had barely progressed and was still in the same place, in the middle of reels of thread and boxes of needles.

This agony lasted two years. Two years is a very long time when you're bored. I was truly impatient to go back to Saudi Arabia. I was sometimes terrified by the idea that we would stay in the United States forever. I had never heard my parents talking about such a possibility but I couldn't stop myself from thinking, and having nightmares, about it.

I was lost in such reflections when one day my mother came to me, after a long, hushed discussion with my father, smiling broadly. She told me what had just been decided and then I too jumped for joy: my mother had said to my father that she couldn't take it anymore and that she wanted to go back to her family, her friends, and her country, and he had agreed that we should return to Mecca. My father would finish his studies alone in Washington.

It was fantastic news. Goodbye America and hello once more to the warm desert sands!

A Marriage Proposal at Eleven

What joy to return to Mecca and the solid old stone house of my grandfather! I plunged myself into a carefree life that followed the rhythm of the sun and the female silhouettes draped in black that slid silently along the pavement. I didn't miss Washington at all—although I certainly hadn't seen the best of it, having been mostly confined to the house or at school. In any case, it was here that I felt at home and I was happy to see my mother smiling again.

She didn't seem to miss my father. He often called her, especially to give orders and ensure that she was carrying out her duties and behaving herself. He never asked after me or wanted to speak to me. I said nothing, but this lack of interest hurt me very much. He did send me toys and games regularly in the mail. Big, anonymous parcels that I unwrapped without emotion, because I knew they never contained a message. Not a note, a photo, a drawing, or a postcard. Just a lifeless, cold object that I hadn't wanted and which meant nothing. I played with these toys, of course, but I was indifferent to them; they signified nothing, not even the absence of my father. They had no soul—their only value was commercial.

I went more and more to my uncle Farid and my aunt for the affection my father did not give me. Their love and kindness largely filled the paternal void, to such an extent that when my father eventually returned from the United States, after a year away, I received him as though he were a stranger. It was wrenching when I learned several weeks later that we were going to move to Jeddah, the great commercial port of Saudi Arabia from which all the pilgrims disembark en route for Mecca. I was very sad at the prospect of leaving my uncle and aunt and the town that I loved so much for one I didn't know. I knew Jeddah was just a few dozen kilometers from Mecca and that my family would often come to see us but I couldn't help thinking of the immense feeling of solitude that had filled me when I was in Washington. But Jeddah was a business center and it was business that called my father there now that he had his qualifications from the United States.

Another town, another style. Jeddah is a modern city and we now lived in a big apartment in a new building. It was beautiful, but I still missed the rough, large stones of my grandfather's home with its vast spaces.

In Mecca, my sister and I had been used to dancing madly in the inner courtyard of the house. My father knew nothing about it. He forbade us from listening to music in this way, but a maternal uncle had secretly given us an old tape player, which we kept hidden under our bed. As soon as our father left, we would rush to get it out, put it on full volume, and then burst into dancing to the latest American, Arab, and Indian music. But one day there was a disaster: my sister put her back out while swaying a bit too energetically. We had to take her to the hospital and admit the cause of the accident to our father. I feared his reaction but he said nothing. He even seemed to regret his ban and feel guilty: his fanaticism had cost his children. Afterward, he actually bought us a new, good-quality cassette player.

Those were the good times. We didn't have as much fun in the apartment as in the house, but at least our father left us the tape player.

He imposed a very strict religious education on us. We had to follow the rules of prayer, but he did accept certain departures from tradition, notably in the way we dressed—a tolerance he had brought back with him from his time in America. One day, while I was rolling around playing on the rug in front of my father, my mother rushed over to pull my skirt down sharply over my little white panties. Seeing her, my father intervened.

"Bah! Let her play without worrying about her dress. There will be time enough for her to pay attention to it in a few years. We don't know what man is waiting for her!"

At the time, I didn't understand what my father meant. Today I do.

At the age of ten, my relations with boys presented no problems. Mixed schools were certainly not the norm, but at home I played with my little male cousins, although under the vigilant and constant watch of my father, who ensured we did nothing he found dubious. That education would mark me, and indeed it still weighed on me when I got married and I had difficulty shedding it on my wedding night with my husband.

This segregation of boys and girls at school occurred naturally; it was part of our education and we experienced it as neither a constraint nor an abuse. Such segregation also existed in certain European countries for a long time without anyone getting upset, and mixed schooling—with which some Europeans still disagree—was only introduced there in the 1960s.

In fact, the real problem in Saudi Arabia was the education of girls, which wasn't really part of our tradition. It took enormous courage for King Faisal to get people to accept it in the 1970s. It wasn't even common then to see boys at school—let alone girls! It was completely unthinkable and went against all our notions of education by upsetting good family order. Women were meant to be married, bring up children, and keep house. End of story. Did they need to read and write to wipe children and knead dough? Female education was an even more incredible luxury when one thinks that in 1970 only nine percent of the entire population was literate. King Faisal's reform therefore put up a lot of backs. Many parents did not understand it and refused to obey, keeping their girls at home. School was not a priority for boys or girls. The king needed iron determination and unwavering authority to change the mindset of many people.

In 1994, some twenty years later, 61.8 percent of the population was literate—70.6 percent of men and 47.6 percent of women [figures from the Saudi government]. Those figures were still too low but nonetheless showed enormous progress. In 1997, the average length of schooling was ten years for boys and nine years for girls: we had almost achieved equality. I think that today we have done so—or perhaps even surpassed it, because many girls are courageous and intelligent and understand that their salvation, freedom, and autonomy are deeply connected to their level of education. They know that the country cannot live forever from its supply of oil and that intellectual emancipation is an irreversible process. In twenty years, Saudi Arabia's GDP is already only a third of what it once was. To augment their income, more and more women will start working outside the home; no more than eight percent did so in 1995, but it is estimated (without official confirmation) that the figure has today more than doubled.

In terms of education, my brothers, sisters, and I had nothing to complain about, even in the 1980s. On the contrary. My father, like my mother, always encouraged us to go to school—sometimes even delivering kicks to our behinds when we lacked enthusiasm.

In our house, school was a family tradition. My grandfather was literate, spoke nine languages, and was a bookseller in Mecca. In the 1950s, one of my aunts had opened one of the two first private schools for girls in Jeddah and the highest dignitaries of the town had entrusted their progeny to her. Against such a background, my father could be nothing but favorable to the wishes of King Faisal.

Indeed, he was so enthusiastic about our schooling that I often cursed his zeal. Most parents grumbled at having to send their offspring to school, but at least two applauded the king's project unreservedly—mine! For my part, I had only lukewarm appreciation for Faisal's directives and his concern that I should learn to count. Frankly, school was not my cup of tea. From the age of ten, I preferred to listen secretly to the Arabic programs of Radio Monte Carlo rather than revise my lessons. It wasn't what I was supposed to be doing, but it could have been worse. Now that I was older, I had a room all to myself in which I could do what I wanted, and every evening I would put my transistor under my pillow, an earpiece in my ear, and listen to the latest records until very late. Perfectly unreasonable for someone who had school the following day, I know.

Result: while my sister, who was in the next room, always jumped out of bed at the first call, bright-eyed and bushy-tailed, my mother would have to come and shake me several times before I got up, grumbling. I often refused to move until my father intervened. I would then get a hiding—but it didn't stop me from tuning in to RMC again the following night. The more I was forced, the less I wanted to go to school. I would even sometimes turn around at the school gates and return to the house; my father was usually told at once and I would pay dearly for my misdemeanors. He wasn't tender, but because we had never connected emotionally I began to get a taste for this rebellion, seeing it as a challenge to his authority. It was unusual for a girl to oppose her father in Saudi Arabia, but I was too young to realize that. My character was expressing itself unwittingly.

This rejection of school had more to do with a refusal of the institution than the lessons themselves. I was not a bad pupil; I liked to read and had acquitted myself quite well in Arabic, but I was lazy, undisciplined, and thought only of enjoying myself. At school, I excelled in the art of organizing breaks to which I even invited the teachers. Every morning, my mother would cram masses of all sorts of cakes into my bag out of fear that my sister or I would go hungry. There was enough to feed an army. My little schoolmates, along with the teachers, quickly developed a taste for these treats, which got them through mid-morning fatigue. The al-Baz sisters' cakes became an institution. I mastered the art of being a young hostess perfectly; it was the subject in which I worked hardest and did best.

Music attracted me as much as school revolted me. Not just what was broadcast by RMC but music in general. From quite a young age, I had learned the electric organ and the oud, which I could play equally well with both my right and left hands. In between practicing somersaults with my sisters, I would sit in front of the keyboard. As for my parents, they already saw me as a doctor. They, particularly my father, would often nag me, "You need to work hard at school to become a doctor..."

All wealthy Saudi families dream of their daughters becoming doctors. Women have to be taken care of by female doctors because it is forbidden for them to be naked in front of a man, even a doctor. Girls are therefore encouraged to study medicine so as to fill this gap.

The future that my father planned for me seemed so remote that I barely gave it any thought. Doctor?—why not, if that made him happy! I didn't doubt that he was serious when he spoke of the profession, but I didn't really listen. Doctor? There was time enough for that; I was still a child. I should be left to my games and to my little girl's dreams.

A little girl... That was what I thought I was until my mother announced one day: "A man has asked for your hand in marriage."

I was eleven years old.

The news overwhelmed me. I didn't believe my mother and was sure she was joking, even though that wasn't like her. I felt myself blushing as red as a beet when, seeing that she wasn't laughing, I asked her to repeat what she had said. I felt that she too was embarrassed when she said dryly, "Yes, you will soon be a woman. It's normal that men are starting to be interested in you. At your age, your grandmother had already received many proposals."

I had felt as though the ground was opening up beneath me. The craziest images ran through my head. A man had asked to marry me... Marriage? But it was only recently that I had been a bridesmaid at weddings myself! A man? What was a man? It wasn't a boy of my age; a man was someone like my father or my uncle Farid! I couldn't be a wife—I could only be a daughter or a niece. Not a wife.

I couldn't understand and looked at my mother despairingly. I was sure she would burst out laughing and say that she'd only been teasing.

Unfortunately, it was no joke. A man, a pilot for an airline company based in Jeddah, had indeed asked my father for my hand in marriage. My father considered his proposal, which seemed acceptable to him. That was why my mother had wanted to prepare me for the news.

Although I soon realized that it was true, I didn't realize the proposal's significance. At eleven, it was impossible to imagine marriage. It was certainly true that Eastern women marry earlier than Western ones, and that during my grandmother's time some men had married young girls, but times had changed and the typical age of marriage for a woman was now seventeen or eighteen. So why break the rule? Why go back in time and marry me at eleven? Did my father want to get rid of me? No, really, the whole thing was impossible and I couldn't understand it.

The next day, when I got back from school, I went directly to my room, where my mother soon followed me. She again spoke to me about marriage.

"This marriage will be very good for you—you're very lucky. Do you realize that? Your future husband is an airline pilot. He won't be at home very often, and you won't see him very much or have to cook. You'll be able to do what you want!"

I began to realize that the matter was serious, but I didn't understand. Obviously, my mother was right: the prospect of not seeing my husband reassured me. Perhaps my life wouldn't change much, and I could continue to go to school and perhaps even keep my room in our house. That would be great. But then why, under such conditions, should I marry? If I never saw my husband, if my life didn't change any more than his did, they should leave me alone and let me grow up in peace with my beloved sister and my friends at school. I was very confused.

I had still not sorted things out in my mind when, several days later, my mother abruptly ended my torment. I'd just gotten home from school and hadn't even had time to put down my bag when she announced: "Your father has turned down the proposal of marriage. It's definitive and the affair is closed."

Curiously, the shock of the refusal was as great as the shock I had felt at the original announcement. A tide of joy swept through me, overwhelming me. Overcome with happiness, I wanted to know more so as to be totally reassured.

"What happened? Did the pilot do something that Daddy didn't like? Did he lie?"

"No, your father made a mistake over your age. He thought you were twelve. When I told him that you were only eleven, he changed his mind. It is too young and you're not yet a woman. We need to wait a bit."

Wait a bit... I quickly did the calculation. If I understood correctly, I had a year of respite; that gave me time to prepare myself, but it was still not long. It was something at least.

I noted yet again just how much interest my father took in me: he couldn't remember my date of birth, a fact that had nearly had a considerable impact on my young life.

My mother declared herself very happy with the news and I knew she was being sincere. But her joy was not just emotional. She had recently opened a shop in town, where she designed, made, and sold dresses. This new activity took a lot of her time and prevented her from watching over the good management of her house as she would have liked. For someone who demanded that every object be in its place and every speck of dust gone, it was a real heartbreak and an unacceptable dereliction of duty. And so she had delegated her powers to me.

We had two employees and I helped my mother in the morning as she rushed around the apartment giving them their instructions for the day. In the afternoon, when I got back from school, I had to check that the orders had been followed and the work done properly. I couldn't forget the least detail. When my mother came in from her work, she would inspect in her turn and woe betide me if there was anything wrong!

This Spartan regime made me grow up, taught me to become a woman and run a house as well as prepare meals for an entire family, which was also part of my duties. But I didn't complain; since learning to cook with my grandmother, I had experienced a real pleasure in being in the kitchen. All the same, I didn't succeed in making all the dishes properly, which my mother didn't fail to point out unceremoniously. I took it on the chin, toughened up, and without even realizing it gradually slid into the role—well before my time—of the married woman that I had almost become.

As the months passed, it became obvious that I wouldn't stay single for long. I had to accept the idea and prepare for my marriage. Hardly had my twelfth birthday passed when marriage proposals began to flood in. I couldn't go to a reception or party without attracting men's desire. Apparently I was pretty. Judging by the mothers flocking to ask my hand for their sons, it must have been true! From what I heard, they admired not only my physique but also the feminine qualities I already possessed. This success gave my father ideas. He who had been ready to marry me off when I was only eleven realized that I was an excellent catch and would have no difficulty finding a husband. He became more and more demanding. There was no more question of rushing into something or selling me off; he would devote time to getting an excellent deal by raising the stakes. I had a certain and sought-after value, which he would be sure paid off!

Between ages thirteen and fifteen, the proposals multiplied. Every Thursday, the traditional visiting day in Saudi Arabia, a procession of mothers would come to the house, taking advantage of the occasion to look at me in detail. This happens in every Saudi family, but my case was particular in that no mother left our house without having spoken of marriage. My mother would pass the proposals on to my father, who would consider them. If they were suitable, he would organize interviews with the suitors and their fathers.

When he met them several days later, the ritual was always the same: the two men would go into the sitting room and sit down on armchairs in front of my father, who would invite them to plead their cause while he observed them carefully. The examination was minute and every detail counted. The suitor had only to turn up in sandals or place one foot on top of the other during the conversation for him to be rejected. Politeness and presentation were primary for my father. When the discussion was over, I would enter the room briefly, a scarf covering my hair, to serve a fruit juice to the three men, thus allowing the suitor to see my face. The protocol was that if he liked me he would, without speaking, offer me a bracelet, watch, or another piece of jewelry. I would then leave the room, still not having uttered a word. My father would make his decision, and if it was positive, then come to ask my opinion.

In the beginning, these parades amused me; the teenager I had become was flattered. I would hide in the apartment to observe my suitors in secret and rank them. The idea of marriage was still not appealing, but it no longer terrified me; in any case, it was inevitable. But as the Thursdays went on, I began to weary of the little game, to the point that I would sometimes lock myself in the bathroom, absolutely refusing to come out before the visitors left. My father wasn't that upset by this. He reprimanded me for form's sake, and threatened me vaguely, but nothing more. As long as he had not yet found the man he wanted for me, he would leave me in peace.

In addition, I brought balance to the household now that my mother had begun working, and he knew it. My departure would create a void in the management of the household that would have to be filled and no one wanted to take over the role. My younger sister did not seem solid or mature enough to take on the responsibility and she didn't have my sense of command or organization. She wouldn't have known how to make the staff respect her.

I took advantage of this respite until the day we received a surprise visit from an important member of our family. A dignitary. He was accompanied by his wife, sons, and daughters: a delegation. Very quickly he asked my father for my hand, on behalf of his son. So off we went with the habitual ceremony—but this time, my father seemed delighted. Faced with his obvious satisfaction, I suddenly dug my heels in. First to annoy him and then because I didn't like the people. I found them unpleasant and hypocritical. And so when my father came to my room to announce, as I had expected, "You'll be glad to know I've found you the ideal husband: handsome, rich, and intelligent," I refused point-blank, using the first pretext that came into my head as justification: "He's got a scar on his nose."

I couldn't have cared less about this scar, but I was using it to oppose my father. The answer was no and that was that. He had asked my opinion, I had given it, and he had to accept it. I rejoiced at returning to my cozy daily routine.

I spent happy days between school, where I never worked hard enough to shine, and the many parties at my friends' houses, which I appreciated infinitely more. There I was really in my element and sparkled. Too much. For, one day, I fell into a trap.

During one of these receptions, two women I didn't know noticed me. They found me pretty and likeable. So far, so good—I had no objection. But the trouble was they had a brother who was looking for a wife.

A Very Desirable Girl

My mother was a little disconcerted when these two women very politely introduced themselves to her in the middle of the party, to confirm that I was indeed her daughter and immediately declare that I would make a beautiful wife for their brother. My mother listened and promised to transmit their request to my father, although she prudently avoided giving our address, asking me instead to leave our telephone number, which the brother in question, Jamal, could call if he wanted an appointment. I sensed it was to do with a new suitor and, weary of all these men, gave a false number.

When we left the reception, my mother told me what the two women had wanted and I admitted my lie to her. She laughed and didn't make any fuss about it, for not a week passed without a new suitor appearing. One more or less made little difference.

Even my pilot had reappeared, but my father seemed unwilling to consider his advances any further. He clearly hoped to find someone better. I was careful not to say what I thought, as my immediate concern was to gain time. As long as the applications were refused, there was no reason to worry. In any case, my parents had made it clear that in the end it would be I, and I alone, who would decide my fate and who would accept or refuse the husband that my father proposed. In this he was only conforming to the prescriptions of Islam, for, contrary to common beliefs, a hadith of the Prophet states that a man cannot marry a woman without her consent.

Unfortunately, the patriarchal culture often overlooks or distorts this text, and in many families the girl's opinion on her marriage is, regrettably, not consulted.

As for me, I took my father's laudable intentions seriously, while remaining on my guard. I wasn't really convinced that he would readily accept a second refusal on my part. I couldn't imagine him again saying to the man he had chosen for me, after a series of minute examinations, "I'm sorry, but I cannot honor our agreement because my daughter does not want to marry you. There is nothing I can do; she decides." I was sure that he would take that as a snub and an insult and an intolerable attack on his authority. In short, I was convinced that my opinion would no longer count for much. It was clear that my father would let me choose only as long as I agreed with him. As he could supposedly only make the right choice, my freedom seemed to me very limited and I sensed that the going would get very rough if I again disagreed.

As long as my father didn't find a suitor to his liking, there was nothing to disagree about. I amused myself by routinely contradicting my mother, just to annoy her, when she found a worthwhile or useless suitor. If she found him handsome, I found him ugly; if she thought he was intelligent, I pronounced him an idiot. This little game irritated her and the angrier she became, the more I enjoyed it. With my father it was different. There it was no longer a game but a real confrontation that I couldn't control. It remained unclear how this battle with the head of the family would unfold.

I was wondering about this when Jamal, after six months of intense research, found my telephone number and called my father, on his sisters' recommendation. I was amused to think that this joke had resulted in something; I'd never thought that the brother would follow up, and it seemed so fantastic that for once I was curious to see the new candidate.

He soon turned up at the apartment, where the joke turned into a farce. Hidden in the window, I watched as he parked his car in front of our home and our big, black, long-haired dog made for his vehicle, barking furiously. Our dog wasn't aggressive, but he was truly huge and intimidating. My suitor, who had just gotten out of his car, hurriedly took refuge in it again, shaking with fear and slamming the door behind him. Then, his nose pressed against the window, he stared at the watchdog, who was running around the vehicle barking for all he was worth. The young man seemed completely panicked and looked around desperately, searching for help that didn't come, and throwing himself back violently every time the beast jumped up to the level of his face—leaving deep scratch marks on the door of the handsome American car that had been carefully polished for the occasion. I didn't dare think of the cost of such damage!

It was several minutes before one of our employees came out of the house to get hold of the dog. The young man then extricated himself warily from the car and I heard him shout several times to our servant, "Have you got the dog? Are you sure? Are you holding it tight?"

As an entrance, it was a success! My potential future husband had made me laugh, and that was something. I continued to watch him secretly while my mother showed him to the sitting room where my father was waiting. The door closed softly on the two men without further incident. I'd enjoyed this introduction and was disappointed when my father did not call me, as he usually did, to serve the traditional fruit juice as a pretext for showing myself discreetly.

It was not a good sign. I sensed that things were not going well and I felt frustrated, excluded from the game.

After more than an hour, my father accompanied the candidate to the door. He let him get into his car before asking me to join him on the threshold of the building so that Jamal could see me from afar.

The tone in which he spoke his first words after the young man left proved that the test had not been conclusive. I was frustrated. Without being able to explain why, I liked this man. In addition to his spectacular arrival, he looked nice. He was tall, young, with a fine face and large dark eyes, and dressed elegantly in an immaculate white burnoose. I felt a revolt mounting within me. I wanted to say what I thought, but held myself back because I didn't know enough yet to give an opinion. My father must have had good reasons for rejecting him.

I didn't have to wait long to find out more: there was a problem in terms of money, my father explained to my mother. I wasn't invited to the discussion, but I made myself small in a corner of the sitting room so as to pick up every crumb of the conversation.

Jamal was an officer in the marines. He was based in Charguia, 1,400 kilometers east of Jeddah. So far there was no problem, even if the distance and the prospect of living in a small town worried me a little. My father didn't seem to see the move as a major obstacle, which didn't surprise me: he wasn't the one who would have to go.

The only problem was that Jamal's father had died and Jamal had been left to look after his whole family single-handedly. This point troubled my father. He feared that such a charge would be too heavy, financially and materially, for my young suitor.

For my part, I found these fears a bit extreme. I didn't see why this Jamal shouldn't be capable of managing the family inheritance well, or even increasing it. But obviously no one asked my opinion on the subject.

Yet this time I really wanted to give it. I'd had enough of people deciding for me. If I was ready to be married, I should also be able to give an opinion about my future.

At first, I brought the subject up with my mother, who confirmed what I already knew of the situation and advised me to conform to my father's choice.

My father's choice! My father's choice! Always my father's choice! Well, I'd had enough of my father's choice and I meant to tell him so. And soon!

That very day, when he got back from the office, I first let him freshen up and then went to join him in the sitting room, where I asked him, without preamble, about his intentions concerning Jamal. His face immediately hardened. That I would dare ask such a question shocked him, but since he was caught off guard, he answered. "There will be nothing further. That boy is not suitable for you."

"Well, I like him. I don't see why I shouldn't marry him."

I said the words clearly, my voice loud and strong. My father paled and seemed short of breath as he said, thinking it would be the last word in the debate, "It is I who decide; do not involve yourself."

"It's my future husband and I have a right to be involved."

Voices were raised, but I didn't yield an inch, and the more my father persisted in his decision, the more I dug myself into mine. At the end of our confrontation, I realized that it was not so much a sudden and excessive passion for Jamal that had motivated me but the delicious enjoyment of opposing my father. This feeling was not new for me, but at that moment it took on a new intensity. I knew that my mother would never dare act like this. I imagined that, following the scene from afar, she feared the worst reprisals for me. But the thunder did not crash around my young shoulders. My father ended the argument, with neither of us having changed our position.

In the weeks that followed this exchange, the atmosphere between my father and me was strained. We both avoided the contentious subject until the day Jamal reappeared.

He called my father to tell him that his post had been changed. He'd been transferred to Jeddah and saw this move closer to me as destiny's affirmation of his choice. Therefore, he sought my hand more than ever. My father refused to give him an appointment, once again detailing the reasons for his decision. Yet Jamal didn't give up. He clung on even tighter. I don't know what his sisters had said to him about me but it must have been convincing, for this soldier mobilized his troops to achieve his goal and launched his whole family into the battle to get my father to agree.

One of his sisters, older than him and then unknown to us, contacted my mother in a bid to reopen negotiations. She wanted her husband to come and see my father. My mother interceded on her behalf and tried to convince my father to accept, reminding him that the interview did not commit him to anything. My father finally gave in reluctantly, but when the day came he performed another, not very honorable, maneuver to try to get out of it. My mother made the mistake of going to sleep several minutes before the time arranged for the meeting and her husband took the opportunity to slip away. When the expected visitor arrived, my mother saw that my father was absent and, unable to explain, could only stammer a few apologies while asking the man to wait in the sitting room.

I watched him through an open door, as was my custom. He didn't seem to take offense at this unexpected absence and even seemed determined to wait however long was necessary.

And in this way he waited three hours in front of the cups of tea that my mother came regularly to top up, declaring that such behavior was most unlike her husband and that he must have been called away by most urgent business. Well brought up, the man pretended to believe it, even worrying, "I hope it's nothing serious. I would be very sorry if something unfortunate has happened."

My mother thanked him warmly for his concern, knowing full well that my father must be drinking tea in a neighboring café or with a friend.

When my father finally came back, his displeasure at seeing the visitor still there was obvious. This time he could not get away and he had to accept the conversation. He was visibly furious. As for me, I hid myself in a corner so as not to miss any of what went on.

After the usual introductions, the man began speaking. He described his family and financial situation and then assured my father that he would be his brother-in-law's guarantor and take on the charge of the family if his brother-in-law were unable to do so. As more powerful persuasion, he described his wealth, his activities, and his income—in such extensive detail that one would have thought he had come for a loan rather than a wife for his brother-in-law.

My father listened but didn't seem at all impressed by the speech. I sensed that he was impatient to put an end to it, and indeed, he brought the interview to a rapid conclusion, showing little enthusiasm as he accompanied Jamal's brother-in-law to the door.

"I'll reflect and let you know my decision."

I knew that he'd already made up his mind: His answer was no.

As soon as he was alone, my father exploded. Reproaching my mother violently for this useless meeting, he told her that he wanted to hear nothing more of the affair.

He was to be disappointed in that, for my uncle Farid took up the baton next.

My mother had in fact kept Farid abreast of the situation for some time and he couldn't understand my father's obstinacy. When he heard of my father's definitive refusal, he decided to step into the breach. He appeared one evening at the house to tell his brother in no uncertain terms what he thought of his methods.

The two men shut themselves in a room for what I later learned was a stormy discussion. Farid reproached my father strongly for his attitude, which he thought shameful and unjust toward the young man. In his opinion, Jamal had shown responsibility and much courage in taking care of his family; instead of being penalized, he deserved to be rewarded. What is more, Jamal's insistence on the marriage proved that he truly cared for me, which wasn't a negligible factor in my happiness—even if I personally didn't really see how one could be so attached to a silhouette glimpsed underneath a veil... In any case, my uncle's argument was very sensible, even if my father didn't necessarily share his views on my happiness. Despite this, Farid's powerful speech bore fruit and made my father a little ashamed of himself. He was shaken.

For several days he tried to let nothing show, but one evening he confided in my mother that, in the end, perhaps the union wasn't so bad after all. I was of an age to be married, so why not to Jamal?

The following day, for form's sake, my father asked my opinion. I was trapped. It was difficult for me to say no to a marriage for which I had clamored so long; yet I was only sixteen, and still a school girl.

It was only in that moment that I realized it was no longer a game.

Until then, marriage to me had been an abstract notion, more an excuse to squabble with my father than anything real. I talked about it all the time, but I didn't see it coming, a little like the imaginary battles one has with an enemy who never actually appears. Now that we were no longer playing, the reality of marriage loomed. I couldn't believe that I was going to commit myself to a man for life—a man I didn't know and whom I had just glimpsed between two doors, but who would be the father of my children. Would he be kind, gentle, attentive, and considerate, or nasty, violent, and aggressive? I had no idea, but I didn't let it bother me too much.

I know that may seem strange, but it was like that: I was reacting according to my culture and my religion. I have a strong faith and I believe that God decides for me. I trust Him. If I failed, I could only blame myself and try to improve by devoting myself totally to the spouse that Allah had chosen. For me, a husband was like a melon bought in the market: they all look the same from the outside, but you have to open the one you've chosen and taste it to know if it's good. Jamal wanted me as his wife so, all right, I would have Jamal, putting my trust in the future.

Love stories are not highly regarded in Saudi Arabia. To talk about "love" would be indecent and immoral. Even if we have heard of the Western custom of Valentine's Day and we know the date of this feast day for lovers, we would never celebrate that way ourselves—although the sale of red roses does explode on February 14 throughout Saudi Arabia because it is customary for pupils in girls' schools to give one to their teacher.

Why would I, who had been educated in this tradition, think for a second about love when I learned I was going to marry? Love was not part of my culture; it wasn't a sentiment I knew. What is more, we girls mixed so little with boys that I found it difficult to imagine such feelings. As a result, this arranged match suited me.

When he heard of my father's unexpected change of heart, Jamal was wild with joy. From that moment, his family, like mine, thought only of the various ceremonies.

My father decided, first of all, to hold the engagement ceremony in our apartment. The engagement is important for Muslims because it occurs in the presence of a judge who sets out the marriage contract and checks and confers the dowry. It is at this occasion that the judicial and material aspects of the union are laid down. It is of extreme, indeed fundamental, importance for the families.

And yet I couldn't help arriving late for this solemn appointment. My father was wild with rage! I am hopeless; I was born to break rules and antagonize my father. And yet I swear I didn't do it deliberately; it was the hairdresser who had delayed things by wasting time curling my hair. At any rate, by the time I came running to the house, my father had condemned me to the agonies of hell.

The judge was already there and everyone was waiting for me. My fiancé had placed a small silver box on a table in the middle of the sitting room, according to tradition. Inside he had placed a copy of the Qur'an, a gold bracelet and necklace, as well as diamond-studded earrings and the ritual presents: two silver coins symbolizing the union, perfumes, sugar candy, and cardamom. Wrapped in silver paper, all these presents recalled ancestral times when the husband's family brought provisions and food to the young couple.

Everything was in order. My father seemed finally satisfied with the turn of events; his anger had disappeared. The formalities over, he even said to me, with something approaching tenderness, "Now you must think about marriage. I will organize it in a big hotel. I want a fabulous feast that you will remember."

A Bride at Sixteen

Three months elapsed between my engagement and my marriage to Jamal. Three months of madness. Caught in a whirlwind, every day I ran from one place to another to prepare for the wedding and organize my future life. I spent hours choosing my wedding dress and then arranging alterations that seemed to me absolutely vital. My mother wouldn't have missed any of these fitting sessions for the world. Her talents as a couturier and her good taste were precious and our common desire for perfection meant that we spent hours in front of the mirror smoothing out a crease or adjusting a veil. I didn't regret all the time we spent, for my white dress was magnificent. I never tired of looking at its long train, which spread in successive waves over the carpet of my room.

My father wanted a beautiful wedding and I thought mine would be, even if I had to battle with the traditions a little. In Saudi Arabia, the ritual of marriage ceremonies varies from one town to another. Each has its customs, and in general the bride and groom conform to them. But my childhood memories of Mecca were too strong and ever-present; my heart was still in my grandfather's house where I had grown up and I desired to marry according to the customs of that city. Anxious not to upset the dignitaries of Jeddah, my father at first seemed reluctant. And then he gave in, for he too felt nostalgia for our old family home, solidly planted in the heart of the Holy City. This problem resolved, he then got down to organizing the reception in a big hotel in town and I have to acknowledge that he did a good job of it.

As the guests began to arrive, I checked one last time that everything was in order. The men would be received in a huge room on the top floor of the hotel, while the women would go outside onto the terrace. Wedding or not, each to their place! The floors were spread with thick carpets, warm and colorful. Everywhere were pretty tables, lovingly decorated, with flowers on each one. My father had ordered hundreds of little crystal boxes, arranged in the form of a cake and containing delicate oriental pastries, and these were distributed on every table. It was an original idea that created a wonderful effect. I savored these decorations as the first notes of music emerged from the terrace, where an orchestra of six musicians were warming up and doing a sound check. My father was also finishing his inspection and then joined me for a last farewell. In several hours, his daughter Rania would no longer belong to him, but would be a woman leaving the hotel on her husband's arm. Waiting for that moment, I joined my friends on the terrace.

There were already many of them there, gathered around the buffet tables. As soon as I appeared, they all ran to congratulate me. They told me I looked superb and that I seemed much older than my sixteen years. I believed them readily. It was what the men who had asked for my hand before Jamal had said. I let myself be taken over by the compliments, enjoying the happiness of the moment.

In Saudi Arabia, all festivities begin at nightfall, when the scorching heat of the day gives way to the softness of the night. Lost in my last thoughts as a little girl, I contemplated Jeddah, which was gently fading below me. Waiters brought the first courses on silver trays, which they placed on the impressive buffet tables. In several minutes, pyramids of food had formed in all four corners of the terrace and on the men's floor. I waited for my husband in the corridor, where he soon joined me. He was also dressed all in white. He took me by the arm and we crossed the thick carpet to a sofa covered in velvet for the traditional photo. Twenty or so bridesmaids and pages gathered at our feet and the women were invited to come and watch the photo celebrating our union. Then everyone returned to their places, accompanied by the sounds of traditional oriental music.

The party lasted the whole night. It was a complete success; we enjoyed tender poultry, meat cooked to perfection, fruit bursting with juice, pastries spilling over with sugar and caramel, and we danced until we were exhausted. It was as fantastic a night as I had ever dreamed. At dawn, escorted by my father, I rejoined my husband. Jamal was solemnly waiting for me in a sumptuous American limousine parked outside the hotel with a white-gloved chauffeur at the wheel. Before climbing into the car I turned for a last time to our guests, massed on the pavement, to give them a big wave. And then the car started.

The rest is something intimate and private. As a Muslim woman I cannot, and do not wish, to say more. That would be inappropriate and contrary to our principles.

After our wedding night, my husband and I settled in a four-roomed apartment, which my mother had helped decorate, in Jamal's family house.

Our apartment was not far from that of my parents and I continued to see my family very often. It was also near my secondary school, and now that the festivities were over, the reality of everyday life resumed: I may have been married before God and men, but to my teachers I was still only a schoolgirl. The change in my status should not interrupt my studies, everyone agreed, including my husband, who encouraged me to continue my schooling. That said, wearing those two hats was not easy. It was strange to have to justify oneself to a teacher during the day and perhaps endure her remonstrations and then to assume the full responsibilities of a married woman, just like the teachers, once I was outside the gates of the school. I often imagined what would happen if I met one of the teachers at a stall or in the supermarket while I was shopping. What a strange situation! How would the conversation go?

"So, Rania, what are you making for your husband for dinner?"

"Chicken and zucchini."

"Very good, but don't forget that you must revise your geography before dinner. Your marks aren't very good."

"I know, miss, I know, but I have so much to do in the house to make my husband comfortable."

"Tell me about it—mine takes up all my time as well..."

Imagining such a surreal dialogue didn't always amuse me. If such an encounter ever happened I knew I would be very ill at ease, that it would embody my growing discontent: I was at home nowhere, neither at school nor in my home, neither among my friends nor with my husband, whom I found distant and cold. I felt a stranger to him, which was surprising given his enthusiasm to marry me. I didn't know how to act. Was I doing too much? Not enough? What exactly did he expect of me? I couldn't sort it out, which disturbed me and affected my school work.

My case was not unique in Saudi Arabia, but it was still exceptional, as I was well aware. As far as I knew, I was the only married schoolgirl in Jeddah. In rural areas, wives of my age were not rare, but women there don't face the same problems. Their status and their way of life barely change after marriage. They have the same domestic tasks and very often continue to live with their parents, where their husband joins them. In a village, people live as a community, with their doors continually open to each other; instead of boundaries, there is a single, shared space in which a young girl can find her bearings once she is married. She is no longer the daughter of one man, but the wife of another, and that is all. She continues to live as before, developing without rupture from an adolescent into a woman and then a mother. Problems of schooling also do not disturb her as, sadly, the literacy of girls is still very limited in our country areas.

It is not the same in the towns. Whether one likes it or not, the fact of going to school keeps one in the world of childhood and the parent–child, teacher–pupil relationship. The pupil-child receives rather than gives; he or she remains the object, not the subject. I was being asked to do both and I no longer knew where I was or how to situate myself.

At school, I never spoke about my husband and did my best to forget my family situation; in order to avoid all questions and so as not to become a freak, I withdrew completely. I shut down and became introverted, which is not in my character. So I became more and more unhappy and increasingly cursed my parents, and also my husband, for having brought me into this situation.

For all the efforts I made, I didn't manage to settle into my relationship. My husband was kind, but to me he remained a man who had simply acquired the right and the duty to touch me. Every morning I forced myself to smile at him when he left, strapped up in his khaki uniform, for the offices at the marine base where he was posted, but my heart wasn't in it. Worse: it was a relief to see him go. I wanted to recapture my carefree adolescence, go to parties, have fun, dance—but instead I had to drag my discontent to school and settle into a life that gave me no pleasure. Especially as my parents persisted in their ambition to make me a doctor, as usual without considering what I wanted. I liked studying literature and art, which wasn't a very good basis for medical studies. But how to explain that? How to express myself without seeming like an eternal rebel? Particularly as I should be grateful to my parents and my husband for allowing me to study. In short, I felt enclosed in a shell that grew ever smaller around me.

While I struggled to come to terms with these problems, which I couldn't succeed in resolving, another event—which I knew was inevitable—only added to my torment. A doctor confirmed that I was pregnant. It is possible to get contraceptives in Saudi Arabia, but their use remains very limited and unthinkable before the birth of the first child. That would be against our family-based culture. It was my duty to give my husband his first child. Given my situation, the news did not overwhelm me with joy; nonetheless, I accepted it. What surprised me more was that Jamal also wasn't brimming over with enthusiasm when he found out he would be a father for the first time. He was certainly not naturally exuberant, but I thought he would show more emotion all the same. He said simply that it was very good news, that he was very happy, that he hoped I was happy and that everything would go well. He was kind, but a little curt. I therefore gave myself up to my exacting vocation as a Muslim woman and carried my child in silence. But I would have to be pregnant both at home and at school, which no one seemed to realize.

In the first months, I managed to hide my pregnancy under our traditional large black robes. There was more elegant attire, but for the moment this suited me. I avoided the rare questions of the more curious by telling them that my family wanted me to dress like this.

Several weeks before I gave birth I decided not to go to school anymore. I told the principal, informing her of the reason for my absence and asking her to keep the news confidential, which she did. I had no reason to be ashamed of my situation, but I didn't want to talk about it.

I was just eighteen when my daughter Rahaf was born. This moving occasion made me forget my troubles. For several weeks, I was enchanted by the little scrap of life who took over my days and distracted me from my boredom. When the time came to return to school, the adorable Rahaf turned into another burden that I had to carry alone. Jamal loved his little girl, but his work didn't leave him any time to look after her. I had to assume responsibility for my daughter, bring her up, arrange for her to be looked after by her grandmother while I went to school, and then feed her, wash her, put her to bed, and rock her to sleep... My whole life consisted of school, shops, and the kitchen. At eighteen, that was hard. Very quickly I again felt depressed. I carried out all my tasks, but they weighed on me more and more. I was burning out.

Jamal realized that I was sad and bored. As the days passed, he took offense at it and also withdrew into a silence that became heavier and heavier. I then discovered that an old relationship was gnawing at his heart and souring ours. His family had hoped that our marriage would pull him out of his depression, but it didn't. Our evenings, spent in front of the television, were gloomy; on Fridays Jamal forced me to accompany him to his family with the baby. These were his only moments of relaxation and pleasure; for me, on the other hand, it was just one more duty. As the dutiful Muslim woman, however, I followed my husband without objection.

My in-laws found me miserable. Jamal's sisters, who had covered me in so much praise, didn't recognize me. They even worried over my health, so sad, absent, and tired did I seem. I reassured them, but inside I was furious at being taken for a killjoy and not being able to tell them the truth: "I'm bored, that's all, I'm bored to death; your brother bores me, school bores me, everything bores me!"

I wanted to shout it out to everyone, to scream it from the rooftops; this would have done me good but unfortunately was not permitted. I wanted to conform to the principles I believed in, even if it hurt me to do so. It was God's will and I should be patient. The big problem was that I didn't succeed in applying these good intentions in every-day life. I wasn't "unpleasant" to my husband but I obviously wasn't pleasant either, even if I defended myself when he pointed it out to me.

To put a bit of color into my life I asked Jamal to buy me cassettes. Lots of cassettes. He didn't like music very much, particularly the kind I liked, but he did as I asked. I then lost myself in the latest sounds just as I had listened to RMC in secret as a child.

It was not unusual for my husband to return from work and find me dancing like a mad thing in front of a mirror. This didn't please him; he didn't get angry, but he remarked, "Do you really have nothing else to do?"

Well, no, I really didn't have anything else to do because everything else, apart from my daughter, got on my nerves. But I was careful not to tell him that. Obedient and docile, I would immediately turn off the music.

We struggled along like this for several months until one evening, when I was again listening to a cassette, this time with headphones, Jamal looked at me for a long time with-out saying anything. He didn't address the least remark to me, but took his newspaper and settled coolly into an armchair. This show of calm was abnormal; I turned off the music, lifted my headphones and sat down in front of him.

He lowered his newspaper and gazed at me fixedly.

"Go back to your parents; I'll come to get you later."

It was a staggering blow. I feared that divorce was imminent. Unable to say a word, I sat there with my mouth open, gasping for air. Yet this idea could have satisfied and relieved me: I was going to be free again, without the constraints of a marriage. Jamal was offering me this liberty, but suddenly it wasn't what I wanted anymore.

That might seem paradoxical, but I had long foreseen this collision between my feelings and my culture and between joy and shame. For that was indeed where the problem lay. Of course the prospect of becoming again the carefree young girl I had been delighted me. But the problem was that I would have to explain and justify it to everyone around me. A divorced woman, particularly with a child, is a black sheep. By repudiating me, my husband was condemning me; he was denouncing me in front of everyone as a bad wife and making me an outcast in our society. What would become of me? How could I explain this failure to my father? He had accepted this marriage under pressure and reluctantly: this separation would prove him right, confirm him in his certainties; far from giving him satisfaction, it would only stir up his regret and fury at having let himself be persuaded, which now obliged him to live, before everyone's gaze, with a separated daughter.

All these thoughts ran through my head while Jamal silently went back to reading his newspaper, pulling with his left hand on the point of his goatee. He seemed surprised when, in a broken voice, I finally asked him: "But why?"

Lifting his eyes, he explained to me without once raising his voice: "Because I've had enough of living with a child-woman, a useless and immature girl. You are not grown-up. I feel like I'm living with my little sister and not my wife, the mother of my daughter. That is your character and time will change nothing. So it is better to put an end to things now, before it's too late."

This analysis was hard, though it contained some truth, even if I found it hard to swallow the accusation of immaturity and even if I wanted to remind him that I hadn't asked him to come looking for me. It is true that by asking for the hand of a young girl whom he has only glimpsed a man takes an enormous risk. It is a major disadvantage of our tradition. Jamal wanted me at all costs, but he didn't know me at all; he might have realized that I was only a child. But his sisters had told him that I was sweet and lively and an opportunity not to be passed up.

I didn't negotiate at all. I saw my behavior as the result of my frustration, a cry for help, a search for enjoyment and a rejection of the boredom that oppressed me, but at that moment I had no desire to either defend or justify myself. I knew it would now be futile. All the same, I asked the classic question, knowing in advance what the answer would be: "Are you sure?"

And the response I expected fell like an axe.

"I am sure. It's irrevocable. You will return home. I will settle things later with your father."

Thrown out. I was being thrown out, and unceremoniously. It only remained for me to pack. Jamal hadn't even given me time to organize my departure. Before I had time to ask, he said, "Go and pack your suitcase right away. As soon as you're ready, I'll drive you to your parents."

I at once thought of our daughter. "And Rahaf?"

"Take her with you. I will also decide about her later. Hurry up."

With these words, Jamal went to our room to change.

Alone, I stared at the telephone for a long time before calling my mother. I didn't know how to tell her about the situation—but I must make up my mind, I thought, for I heard Jamal bustling about. I slowly lifted the receiver.

My mother listened to my tale in silence. Her reaction surprised and comforted me. Rather than the reproaches I had expected, she seemed almost happy to have me return to the nest. In any case, she sympathized with me and reassured me: "Come quickly, my little girl, all that will sort itself out. It doesn't matter. I will warn your father and prepare your room for you and Rahaf."

My Mother, My Friend

Jamal didn't utter a word as he drove me back to my parents. He concentrated on the road and avoided looking at me. Only Rahaf broke the silence with her burbling. She was too little to understand what was happening. I had simply told her that we were going to spend a few days with her grandmother and she seemed happy at the prospect. Poor child. If only she knew how our lives were crumbling. I was under few illusions. I had a powerful sense that this separation prefigured a much more serious one. I feared the worst: a definitive separation. I wondered whether I was really a bad wife and mother. Thrown out, demeaned, and shamed: this was what I had to accept without a word. Yet that was not even what upset me; for the moment, I was much more concerned with the consequences than the causes. My life was broken. I was humiliated and would never be able to look my parents in the face again. The proud and rebellious young girl who had delighted in opposing her father was today trembling at the idea of seeing him. This failure would mortify him and he would make me pay for it.

When we arrived at my parents' house, Jamal wasted no time. He placed the two suitcases in which I had hastily stuffed our clothes on the sidewalk and left, not even looking at his daughter.

As soon as I appeared, my mother came toward me with open arms and clasped me to her chest. This time the emotion was too much and I began crying. I didn't try to hold back the tears; I felt a curious comfort in being able to weep openly. My sisters came running in their turn and everyone sobbed.

My mother had prepared my room—my teenager's room that I should never have left so early, with the photos of my favorite singers still pinned to the walls. My mother and sisters began unpacking my suitcases, putting my things away in the drawers while telling me everything they were doing. I didn't hear them; it didn't interest me. I was far away.

I was drinking tea with my mother when my father came back from the office. He immediately came over to me smiling and tapped me affectionately on the shoulder. Not a reproach nor a criticism, though I felt that he was ill at ease and couldn't bear the whole business, even if he didn't want to show it.

The atmosphere over the following days remained heavy. Conversations with my father were polite but brief. Just touching on the subject, without elaborating, my mother admitted that he was annoyed. He had never been gregarious, but now he withdrew even more, avoiding receptions and family parties for fear that someone would ask the dreaded question: "What's become of Rania?"

Rania? What had become of her did not interest him. Only his own fate was of importance. His dignity had been affronted. A repudiated daughter—what shame in front of his friends. How would he explain this situation? That was his only concern. Even though he had never been very interested in my marriage, in his heart, my father knew that it was not a good one, and that I wasn't the only one at fault. He had understood that the day that Jamal had said, to blame me, that I was a poor cook; my father was in a good position to know that that was not true. But today that was not the problem. The circumstances mattered little; only appearances counted and I had been repudiated by my husband, which made my father extremely uncomfortable.

Admittedly, my mother was not very comfortable with her friends, either. When she received them at home, she avoided speaking about me even though everyone wanted to know more, to express their pity and to pick up bits of gossip for the next social gathering.

I found the situation unbearable. With every passing day, I blamed myself a little more. I cursed myself for making my parents unhappy and depriving my mother of the evening receptions that she loved so much but which my father now refused her more than ever. I was convinced that my brothers and sisters also suffered from the oppressive atmosphere. No one laughed in the house anymore; it seemed inhabited by a spirit of death. It was all my fault and everyone was waiting for just one thing—for Jamal to show up and take me back.

I shut myself up in my room for hours at a time to try to understand what had happened. I began writing a diary in which I confided all my impressions. I went over the same memories again and again, blaming myself for such-and-such an attitude, such-and-such an unfortunate word. I felt guilty, stupid, and useless. I was ruining the lives of my whole family.

Over the course of the next weeks, I fell into a total depression. I stopped eating, I had terrible headaches, and was visibly losing weight. I would constantly watch out the window, convinced that Jamal was going to come. I watched even at night, hoping to make out his car in the beams of headlights that swept across the street. I couldn't sleep. In the morning at breakfast my mother would find me exhausted over my cup of tea.

She worried about my depression, which was getting worse. She wanted me to find activities to occupy me, but unfortunately I had the heart for nothing, which was the very nature of my illness.

After two months of silence, Jamal finally came to the house. When I saw him arrive, I was sure that he had come to get me. In fact, he had simply come to take Rahaf with him. Never mind—I saw it as a first step and I was certain that I too would soon go back to our apartment. I clung to this hope and was happy. The whole house seemed relieved that the problem was resolved.

Alas, the days succeeded each other and nothing happened. Jamal didn't reappear. I called him and begged him to go back on his decision. I apologized and promised to do everything he wanted if only he would take me back and I could find peace again. His only response was: "I'll reflect on it. I'll see."

Several days later, while I was resting, someone rang at the door. My little brother Ala went to open it and I heard talking. Intrigued, I went to see who the visitor was, but the moment I arrived, Ala closed the door again. I saw him slip a piece of paper furtively into his pocket. I asked him who it was.

A little embarrassed, he replied, "Jamal. He wanted to see Daddy."

"And the paper?"

"It's nothing."

I didn't believe a word. I insisted and threatened him until he finally gave it to me. I unfolded the document. A single word jumped to my eyes: "divorced"!

Without even taking the time to put on my veil, I ran into the street. I caught Jamal and seized him by the collar, shaking him: "Why did you do this?"

At that moment my brother and my uncle Farid, who had been alerted, arrived. They tried to hold me back and

calm me down. Suddenly everything around me was spin-
ning and became blurred. I fainted. Jamal ran to his car and
disappeared. I was taken to the hospital, where the doctors
diagnosed a cerebral hemorrhage. This would leave its mark;
for eight years afterward I suffered epileptic fits.

After this incident, I fell into a deep depression. My
mother did everything to try to help me shake it. I should
have enrolled at the university and begun medical studies in
radiology, the path my family and teachers had chosen for
me. But the mishaps, my hospital stay, my convalescence,
the shock of separation, divorce, and the move had all upset
my plans. I had done nothing about it and no one in my
family had thought about my enrollment. And so the university year had started without me, which didn't help my state
of mind—although the doctor said that I wouldn't have been
able to study in my condition anyway.

My spirits at their lowest, this forced inactivity nonetheless had a good side: it brought me closer to my mother. We
talked at length in my room or in the sitting room, something we had never done before. A strange chemistry
occurred between us and our bond tightened. We'd had to
wait nearly twenty years! We became friends and then even
companions.

To try to get me out of my depression, my mother shared
strange confidences with me. Little by little, she told me of
her troubles, her disappointments, her frustration, and her
marital problems. I would never have guessed that this
haughty, cold, and determined woman might have been
unhappy. The mask she wore hid her distress. She confided
all this to me for the first time because she recognized
herself in me: she too had suffered in silence from the
authority and intolerance of my father. She too had always
given in and swallowed her dignity without complaint
because the man is supposed to be all-powerful. My mother
had found hope and salvation in her work; that was where

she affirmed her identity and saved her honor, refusing to live like a slave or a servant on crumbs from his table. Seeing me lost, she gave me her secrets so that I could find my way again and not lose hope.

I knew that my mother's family, originally from India, had arrived in Saudi Arabia from the north after a long and difficult journey. My mother spoke Urdu, a language derived from Hindi and mixed with Persian. She had taught it to me when I was very small and I spoke it fluently, although until then I had never heard it used and thought little about it. Suddenly I understood that through this language my mother had handed down to me her cultural heritage and the identity that had been stolen from her—the past that had been despised, ignored, and trampled underfoot.

"I have also suffered, my child. A lot. My parents and grandparents were very courageous. They had to fight hard to get here. But they were much less wealthy than your father's family, as I was quickly, and unceremoniously, made to understand. I have always been considered 'inferior.' I was lucky enough to be pretty, otherwise..."

Through this brutal revelation, the source of my mother's pride was suddenly revealed. For years she had suffered in silence. She had hid her resentment and used her strength to protect herself and build her inner life. She had created a world for herself amid a society that was indifferent to her.

She sat opposite me, her head slightly turned and the sunshine illuminating her fine features. I looked at her as I never had before. She was beautiful—that had saved her, but also deprived her of freedom. That was the message she was giving me today: I shouldn't accept the unconditional authority of a husband but should exist in my own right and stop blaming myself for the divorce. Like her, I should find the strength to be free within myself.

My mother explained further: "It's thanks to my career that I dare look at myself in a mirror. When I opened my dress shop, your father saw only the financial aspect—the only one he recognizes. But for me, creating those designs gave me an existence. Making them brings me much more than a bit of money: this work carries my signature. It is my recognition and assures my material but also intellectual independence. Now I am no longer the shadow of Yahia al-Baz; I am Nawal and I am well and truly alive. Believe me, it is through work that a woman liberates herself. It is her sole means of escaping slavery and avoiding becoming a mindless animal. Work, Rania, I beg you—that way, you will at least find freedom in your own mind."

This new relationship with my mother helped me get through this difficult time. She provided some answers for me, reassured me, and proved that I wasn't the only woman to feel oppressed.

One day she confided that she was furious at not having been able, for years, to organize parties as she would like. My father was always opposed to it. She had to fight all the time for him to give in and allow her to give a few. My mother dreamed of a house in constant movement, resounding with shouting, laughter, and singing—everything my father hated. Listening to her, I imagined what my life with Jamal would have been like and I began to think that this divorce perhaps had its good side.

I still asked myself why a woman who had been rejected by a man was automatically rejected by the whole of society. Why should the divorced man continue to live normally? No one held it against him. These fundamental questions helped me stop blaming myself. I began to realize that I wasn't solely at fault. I had to forgive myself.

I was thus slowly beginning to pick myself up when Jamal finally left our daughter at the house. From that day, by tacit agreement, we would take turns having her.

Getting Rahaf back, even partly, was a huge source of happiness for my mother and me. The return of my daughter motivated me and gave me back a taste for life. I made new goals for myself and thought, above all, about returning to my studies. I wanted to be able to provide fully for my daughter in the future, have a real career, and a respectable status. I could not miss another start of the university year. But the facility where I would begin my radiology studies was 20 kilometers from Mecca, and 100 or so from Jeddah. I would therefore have to be in residence. Who would look after Rahaf?

There weren't that many possibilities: my little girl would stay in the family home and my mother and sisters would take care of her.

Of course it was hard for me once again to leave my child, as well as my family and the apartment in Jeddah where I had finally found my bearings. But I had to accept it. I had no choice.

Although I was twenty years old, on the first day of university I was as anxious as a child going to school for the first time. I fiddled nervously with my veil as I visited the campus.

The residence hall where I would live was several hundred meters from the school of medicine. It was composed of small three-story buildings and surrounded by gardens, giving it a pleasant appearance. I shared a suite with seven other women students whom I met there for the first time. They seemed nice. We each had a room and every floor had a communal kitchen at the end of a long corridor. The atmosphere seemed friendly, but I felt alone and depressed. Another new existence! I'd had too many in the last four years.

Fortunately, my spirits soon lifted. The community life was a pleasant surprise. Our little group bonded quickly and we became companions, happy to be there. I rediscovered my schoolgirl spirit, which did me enormous good. I emptied my mind by indulging in hilarious, contagious laughter. I was getting rid of bad memories and existing in the present. I even glimpsed a happy future for myself.

My renewed vitality enabled me to reclaim control of my daily life. My energy returned and spread beyond myself; a natural leader, I automatically came to the fore of our little group and my friends even pushed me into being the head of operations. I ruled everybody, as our supervisor rapidly realized—although she didn't mind at all; on the contrary, she was delighted. Instead of policing us, she would often come to our parties. She was a very nice woman, an Egyptian who had lost her husband when she was very young. Alone with two children to bring up, she'd had to leave her country to find work. Life was not always easy for her and it did her good to relax with us. My decisions sometimes alarmed her a bit, but she put up with them.

One day, for example, I decided to fix our shower problems. We had many taps and bathrooms on our floor but for some reason, the water no longer came up to the third floor and we had to fill buckets, cans, and jugs from the floors beneath to have water. It was a pain for the kitchen, but for the shower it was unbearable—a real gymnastic effort. We spilled water everywhere, which had to be mopped up afterward. I was fed up with the situation and found a solution that I offered to my friends: "It's hot and there are hoses outside the building, so we should take our showers there!"

What had I said? The girls were horrified. "What? Outside? In the garden? Naked in front of everybody? You're completely mad!"

"Why? There aren't any boys—it's just us. We can see each other naked without any problem..."

But the seven girls huddled together and gathered their veils fiercely around themselves.

"Absolutely not, no question!"

Dear, dear! What a to-do! I had really touched on a sensitive spot: our relationships to our bodies, our nakedness, and our wretched modesty. This time the girls didn't follow me but resisted, seeming truly shocked. I held fast and argued the point. I suggested that they could shower with a light tunic on. It wasn't very convenient but it would work. They agreed, but they still weren't convinced. The problem was in their heads. Everything that was at all connected with sex was taboo. Our girls, like our boys, are very troubled about the subject; you only had to see my fellow students huddling together and laughing inanely when they saw two dogs mating in the garden to understand.

What I was proposing went against their education and their culture. Too used to hiding their bodies, these girls ended up denying them or concealing them as though they were shameful. I explained to them that the body is beautiful and healthy and that it had to live, move, and breathe, but my speech did no good. Faced with such resistance, I declared that in any event I would go and shower in the garden and I invited them to come and observe that it was more convenient than sprinkling oneself with a jug. With these words I took a towel and some soap and went down.

Hardly had I arrived on the ground floor when I heard a cavalcade of footsteps and shouts of laughter on the stairs. All the residents of the third floor had come to watch the extraordinary sight of a shower in the open air and in public. As I seized the nozzle, I noticed that some of the girls had brought towels and soap but were still hesitating. Soaping myself all over, wrapped in a light material, I shouted out to them, laughing:

"It's nice! It's better than up there!"

Then I saw another student get undressed, then two, then three, and soon we were all laughing like idiots and spraying each other with great jets of water, under the bewildered eyes of our supervisor, who didn't know whether to applaud or to run and alert the university authorities. In the end she opted for the former, enjoyed the spectacle and from then on called me "the flower"—a reference to being watered. This nickname stayed with me.

When we got back to our room, the conversations ran riot. My friends were overjoyed; they sang and enjoyed themselves, having completely forgotten their reservations, which they'd shed entirely. The outdoor shower had liberated them. I was happy for them and I too savored a strange feeling of freedom and, I admit, of victory.

From then on, these showers in the garden became commonplace. When I had first touted this idea, it had seemed weird and shocking to them and some of my friends had felt as though they were undergoing some dangerous transformation—and now here we were having our communal shower outside our building before we said our prayers. This practice obviously did not go unnoticed! The news quickly did the rounds of the university residences and eventually reached the principal. She had nothing to say about it. At least it absolved her from having to deal with the chronic adequacy of the sanitary arrangements. Everyone was happy. On the other hand, the name of Rania al-Baz, Rania the troublemaker, was inscribed indelibly in the principal's mind; she knew that I was the cause of this innovation and, even if she'd accepted it, I was put on the list of girls to watch.

Rightly, in fact, because I would soon launch a new battle, much more serious in its consequences as this time it concerned the problem of the veil.

For security reasons, the university authorities had decided to give each student an identity card with a photograph of her uncovered face. This provoked a great outcry, and what surprised me most was that it was the girls themselves who rose up against this measure as contrary to their culture. Not only did they refuse to have the photo taken, but they rejected even the idea of an identity card. I found it hard to follow them in that. Knowing the hold I had over my companions, the principal called on me to help her persuade them of the need for this photo.

I understand and accept the wearing of the veil, which is part of our tradition and history. I don't see how women could be forced to give it up. But on the other hand, we also have

to take account of changes in our society and adapt to circumstances, particularly in light of events such as September 11th.
In Saudi Arabia, which stripped bin Laden of his Saudi citizenship, the threat of terrorism is very real. I found it
irresponsible to refuse security measures, although my friends
didn't want to hear about it. I repeated in vain that it was our
leaders, those who were responsible for the sacred Black
Stone of Mecca (the Ka'aba) themselves who demanded this
new measure—they wouldn't budge. No photo without a veil;
indeed, no photo at all. I realized then that it wasn't the Saudi
authorities who were the most attached to the traditions that
the West thinks belong to another age, but the people themselves. As I was beginning to realize, asking people to open
their minds is a risky business. My roommates thought a lot
of me, but this battle I was fighting in the name of security
seemed suspect to them. They didn't understand what was at
stake, seeing an attack on their beliefs where there was just
concern for their protection.

We debated the point over and over. I had to argue
cautiously, without ever shocking or provoking. It wasn't
easy but, little by little, I scored points. In any case, the
university authorities were clear: the ID card was obligatory.
Those who refused to submit to it would not be allowed in
the facility. My argument therefore became purely theoret-
ical—and I became even more determined. It hurt me to see
my friends suffocating in the constraints of outdated, poorly
understood traditions.

That said, several days later, when the identity cards
were underway, I almost started to agree with my friends
when a security manager in one of the university's administrative offices leered at me: "You're the prettiest!"

I found the remark inappropriate and astonishing. "How
do you know? We're always veiled!"

"I've looked at all the photos!"

I couldn't bear the idea that these men had pawed over
our photos to compare our looks. I didn't reply, but said to

myself that sometimes this veil was a good thing.

Shortly afterward, another incident brought me up against a security officer. To make phone calls, we had to leave the residence hall because it had no cell-phone reception. The public phone booth was just beyond the security point where we now had to show our IDs. Despite the cards that we all now carried, the guards discriminated by handing out authorizations as they liked, giving some girls the right to go and telephone and refusing it to others.

And so one day a guard prohibited me from going out when he had just let another girl go. I had figured out what was going on: before getting the green light, she had flirted a little with the man, while I refused to take part in such games. I told the guard as much and he took it very badly and barred my way. Very quickly, voices were raised. Drunk with fury, I made off immediately to the principal to denounce such activities.

Sanctions fell quickly. The guards knew who was responsible and I realized that it would not be in my interest to forget my ID. But their revenge did not stop there. One morning, a friend came to warn me: "Have you seen the wall surrounding the residence?"

"No, why?"

"Go and look."

Curious and slightly worried, I hurried to the wall. Long before I got there, I saw it: My name, written repeatedly and accompanied by obscene insults, all over the wall, without any commentary or explanation. It was impossible to miss this foul graffiti. I was sickened and deeply hurt. It is very hard for a young woman to see herself called all the names under the sun in front of everyone. I immediately ran to my room, threw myself on my bed and cried. The stupidity and injustice of it was outrageous. My friends comforted me; they already knew, as did the whole campus. I had acquired a celebrity that I willingly would have foregone. I feared above all that it would alienate the principal.

But no! I had been noted for my rebellious and militant side, but on the other hand the dean of the university was always declaring that my class was the best there had been for a long time, and that largely made up for it. Even if I was much less prominent in class than in the residence hall, I was included in the excellent general standard and the joyous mood of my year. Taking advantage of the serious-ness and the warm atmosphere of the class, I cut a good figure in my department. It was fortunate that the atmos-phere was so good and the other girls so nice because I still wondered what I was doing in radiology.

I hung on because I was thereby guaranteeing my free-dom through work, as my mother had advised me. Fair enough, but I had to work very hard to do so because the course really didn't interest me. I still preferred literature. I would spend long hours in my room writing poems and little stories and I remained convinced that this was my true voca-tion. Nonetheless, despite my lack of motivation, I had embarked on radiology and was determined to try to see it through. A conversation I overheard one day between two of my teachers didn't make things easier. Like most of our teachers, they were Indian and like all their compatriots, only the good salaries had attracted them to Saudi Arabia. Other than that, they didn't like the country much, as I was about to find out.

The two men were speaking in Urdu, without worrying about me. Unluckily for them it was my mother's language and I understood them perfectly. What I heard disgusted me. One of the teachers was explaining to the other, who had just arrived at the university: "Don't bother yourself: all these students are useless and in any case we shouldn't teach them too much, or they'll steal our jobs. Give second-rate lessons, that's enough, and don't worry, no one will know..."

These words were humiliating and unacceptable from the mouth of someone paid by the university. I couldn't stop myself from intervening. The two teachers were stunned when I said to them in perfect Urdu, "You don't have the right to say that or to act in that way. Your attitude is scandalous and I'm going to notify the authorities."

And with that I marched off to the principal's office, who saw me almost immediately. I told her what had happened. She listened to me attentively, noted the names of the teachers and then concluded, giving me a strange smile, "Thank you for informing me. I will call these two teachers and ask them to explain themselves. But tell me, Miss al-Baz, it seems that nothing can happen in this university without you being mixed up in it—you're a real lightning conductor!"

This observation was inevitable and I was forced to agree with it. Embarrassed, I stammered, "Yes, but it's chance; I don't do it deliberately."

My principal didn't seem convinced, but we left it there. I went back to my hall, satisfied that I had reported this unpleasant conversation, but recognizing all the same that something within did urge me to push beyond the boundaries.

To prove this point, for some time I had regularly been playing truant with two of my roommates. Rather than going to class, we would take a taxi and visit one of my cousins in Mecca; it wasn't good, but it gave us a bit of fresh air. Being in the university 24 hours a day ended up being a bit oppressive. Sometimes I wanted to see other places and other people and so my two friends and I would go to Mecca to relax and have a change of scenery. Sometimes we even stayed the night with my cousin and only went back to the university in the morning, which was strictly forbidden for residents. Fortunately we had our good supervisor on our side, who closed her eyes to all our misdemeanors as long as we remained discreet.

Every Wednesday evening I would also go back to Jeddah, where I would stay until Friday afternoon. It was good to spend two days with my family and above all with my little girl. I missed Rahaf so much that a mad idea occurred to me: what if I brought her back with me to the residence hall? I talked about it first to my roommates: no problem. On the contrary, the prospect of having a doll to play with enchanted them. All that remained was to get the indispensable agreement of our floor supervisor. The negotiations did not take long. Not only did she accept that Rahaf should stay with me, but, in return for a small salary that came in handy for her, she agreed to look after my daughter during the day, introducing her to the guards as her own. The security guards would never question her. A minor employee could do what she wanted with her child, it was of no interest to them.

This arrangement was wonderful. Every evening, before two class review sessions, we would pamper and cosset Rahaf, who was in seventh heaven with so much attention. Eight mommies just for her! If the principal had realized that her university was also a nursery...

And so we lived as a family until the end of the university year. But when I went back to Jeddah, my father announced that I wouldn't return to the university residence the following year. He thought the clandestine presence of my daughter in the residence hall was unhealthy and couldn't last. An apartment was free in my grandfather's house in Mecca where we had lived when I was a child. I would settle there with my daughter. My uncle Hassan, of whom I was so fond, lived just above and my aunt had agreed to look after Rahaf during the day when I was at the university.

The prospect of returning to this old, warm house, full of memories, and above all rejoining my uncle and aunt, filled me with joy. Only the idea of separating from my little band at the university pained me a little, but I realized that life would be more comfortable for me and above all for my child in Mecca. That, at any rate, was what I believed.

Several weeks later, when I was alone in the apartment in Mecca, on the ground floor of the family house, I rediscovered with great delight the garden of my childhood games, with all its forgotten scents and noises. I saw Rahaf open her eyes wide with wonder at the sight of it. The place was too big for us, but I didn't complain; at least everything worked here and I didn't have to shower with a hose. When the moment came to put away my and my daughter's things, it truly sank in, for the first time, that I was going to live alone. I asked myself whether over time that isolation would not weigh on me.

Such were my reflections. I discovered, however, that I wasn't the only one to wonder at my situation. I hadn't realized that it was totally atypical in Saudi Arabia. A woman alone with a child—what could she be? Mentally ill? A depraved woman rejected by her husband and family? What was certain, in any case, was that she had a doubtful past and was not desirable company. I rapidly realized that I was suspect in the eyes of my neighbors and that they were ostracizing me. Yet they knew who I was; most of them had known me as a child. Both my uncle and aunt had explained to them that I was studying 20 kilometers away and that it was more convenient for me to stay in the house with my daughter from whom I didn't want to be separated—but it didn't make any difference; no one believed them and everyone pointed the finger of shame at me. I wasn't expecting this and it was not pleasant. Luckily, Hassan and his wife were there to protect me. Without them, I could not have stayed; the pressure would have been too much. I experienced not just suspicion, but hostility.

This experience enabled me to see the gulf that separates us from the West. Here in the East a woman alone with a child is judged harshly and is supposed to take refuge among her family, not expose her failure indecently to everyone. The single-parent family is not common in our country. That said, because of these sacrosanct principles, the family structure has been preserved, which is surely preferable for the development and well-being of the child and even the mother. These are two different concepts of society.

For my part, I didn't have a choice, which was what my neighbors didn't understand. I had to learn to live with their dirty looks. The university occupied me enough so that I didn't suffer too much, but I can only imagine what they must have thought when, on top of everything, my ex-roommates came to have fun and sleep in my apartment. For them, my apartment was a godsend that allowed them to escape occasionally from the university.

This parenthesis in my life lasted a year. After that I went to pursue my university career in a new school of medicine that had just opened in Jeddah.

Rahaf and I returned to my parents' home.

A Television Star

At first I was happy to go back to my parents in Jeddah. I brought a breath of fresh air to my mother and we spent many hours talking while we walked in town with Rahaf. Our relationship had completely changed. My mother had borne her secret in silence for too long and finally being able to share it comforted her. For my part, her unaccustomed tenderness also comforted me and I was able to think of the future with a greater sense of serenity. The only question I avoided asking myself was about my aptitude for radiology. There was still time to see. The only dark cloud on the horizon was the fact that my father did not share our enthusiasm. His disliked this new living arrangement and was often grumpy, irritable, and unpleasant toward his granddaughter.

His attitude hurt me for, like all children, Rahaf sought affection from her grandfather. But he repeatedly rejected her advances. Worse still: my father often lost his temper over her, declaring that she was costing him a lot of money. He found it abnormal to have to pay for her food while she lived under his roof and continually repeated to my mother that she should stay with her father all the time. Since Jamal had asked for the divorce, my father thought he should take permanent care of his daughter, as fathers in that situation generally did.

I felt ashamed of my father when I heard him talking like this. As if feeding a child could put a strain on our budget! My father didn't love his granddaughter and that was all there was to it, even if my mother continued to assure me that this wasn't true. She explained that he acted like this because he was angry with Jamal. I understood that she was trying to keep things calm, but I didn't believe a word of it. No one in the house was fooled. My sisters and brother supported me and we ganged up against our father, who often found himself isolated. We ignored him; he was a stranger among us. One day, when Rahaf had left the house to go to Jamal, everyone took on a funereal air, to such an extent that my father eventually asked, "Why do you all seem so sad?"

The stinging response came: "Because we miss Rahaf."

My father reeled visibly and turned away without comment. Several days later when Rahaf was once again with us, she went to watch a cartoon on television. I opened the door of the sitting room to make sure she was being good and, to my great surprise, saw her sitting on my father's knees in front of the screen while he gently stroked her hair. I was overcome with joy; it was a marvelous moment. Even if my father was as distant as ever with me, at least he spared his granddaughter that coldness, and that was the important thing. The house became cheerful again and I could go back to my studies with a clear mind.

There was a different atmosphere in the new university department in Jeddah and it was nothing like my life as an external student in Mecca. There was none of the "school-girls running riot" of before; the general tone was much more serious, scholarly, and mature and it made me realize that I was heading for a professional life. It also opened my eyes by serving as a cruel reminder that the direction chosen for me was a dead end. Now I could see what was waiting for me and I panicked. What was I doing in radiology? It didn't suit me at all. I couldn't imagine spending my life behind an X-ray machine; it was unthinkable. I dreamed only of poetry and music. But as much as the prospect filled me with dread, I saw no escape. I was stuck. I couldn't deliberately fail my exams—that wouldn't be honest toward my family, and in any case what good would it do me? I wouldn't have my radiology qualifications and would have nothing else in their place. A great situation!

And so, however difficult it was, I put aside my artistic ambitions and forced myself to take an interest in the course I was following. When you don't have what you like, you have to like what you have, they say. I tried to follow that dictum to give myself courage, but this intellectual cover-up didn't prove very satisfying. When I got home I didn't get out my course notes or my medical books, but the school exercise book in which I had for years jotted down my writings. That was where my happiness lay: I would line words up, assemble them, make them speak and give them life. I could stay writing like that for hours.

Alas, very soon afterward, serious health concerns took me away from both my poems and my lectures. The epileptic fits that had until now been relatively rare (and discreet) began to increase. From now on I was liable to lose consciousness without warning and be shaken by violent fits. These fits were ruining my life.

The first time it happened was at breakfast. I suddenly felt dizzy and then blacked out. When I regained consciousness, I made out the faces of my mother and sisters above me; I saw the worry in their faces. I was completely unaware of what had happened to me and my mother explained as she bathed my face in cool water. I saw a doctor who of course diagnosed epilepsy, the problem that had been in the background since I had split up from Jamal—indeed, I couldn't help but connect my ex-husband to my torment. I held him responsible for the situation; I hated and cursed him.

Seeing my anxiety and fear, the doctor tried to reassure me, "Don't worry, it could be an isolated incident. There is nothing to indicate that there will be others."

Unfortunately, there would be others. Many.

Several days later at the university I was again suddenly overtaken by dizziness. In the middle of a lecture, I fell like a stone, my arms and legs stiffening while I was shaken with convulsions and saliva frothed out of my mouth in front of my horrified classmates and teachers. I was immediately rushed to the infirmary.

When I came to, I was mortified. I felt guilty of I didn't know what crime and blurted out apologies. My father came to get me and take me to the house. That evening with my parents I decided to go for in-depth medical tests.

I don't know how many times I went to the hospital. Far from reassuring me, the doctors appalled me; their diagnoses collided with and contradicted each other. Some talked about a tumor while others spoke of a hereditary defect and yet others insisted it was epilepsy. The latter were right, but while waiting to know I was riddled with doubt, fear, and anxiety, for the fits became more and more frequent, each time plunging me deeper into despair.

I could not bear to think of how I looked. The knowledge that I had had a seizure and laid on the floor in front of everyone was unbearable. I knew I was pretty, for everyone told me that often enough, and my pride took a serious blow. A pretty girl cannot become a spectacle in this way, writhing on the floor like a worm. It was perhaps vain and immature, but I felt degraded and humiliated by these public fits. I judged them unworthy of me and this psychological aspect damaged me as much as the illness itself.

My spirits were again flagging. At the very moment when I had been trying to rebuild my life, I was once again plunged into uncertainty, overcome by the horrible feeling that I was ruining my family's lives and giving them nothing but problems.

Several times during my fits, my father had carried me on his back to his car to drive me to the hospital. I was mortified to learn this. He suffered from cardiac problems and could have lost his life in these efforts. I begged him not to do this anymore. I saw that I was becoming more and more dependent on my family and friends, which was intolerable for me.

And yet everyone was extremely kind. At university, my friends surrounded me, watched over me and would rush over at the least warning sign. The teachers were just as watchful and attentive—as those at Mecca had been when I'd had similar problems there. The principal of the university, a doctor, had even suggested that I stay with her so that she could watch over my health.

This proposal was touching, but I preferred to stay with my friends, whose warmth and friendship were precious to me. Being surrounded by my family was also invaluable in these difficult circumstances.

Conscious that I was complicating everyone's lives, I made an enormous effort to appear cheerful and humorous all the time. It wasn't easy, but I clenched my teeth and forced myself to make the whole house laugh by making jokes, gags, and tricks. My heart wasn't really in it and everyone knew that deep down I was miserable, though they each tried to cheer me up.

Notable among these stalwart encouragers was Abu Sultan, one of our neighbors and a friend of my parents, an older man who thought of me as a daughter. He was a radio commentator and we'd had a special connection ever since he had discovered my passion for writing. One day, seeing me write in a school notebook, he had asked, amused, to read what I was writing. When he put it down he said to me admiringly, "That's very pretty. You have talent—you're gifted in writing. I didn't know."

He also loved books and our mutual love of beautiful texts bound us together. It had even become a sort of ritual: as soon as I arrived to visit him he would glance at the door of his study, swearing, "You've come to filch my books again..."

It was true that I had carried out real raids on his library, to the point that he now forbade me from taking more than one book at a time, knowing very well that I would succeed in leaving with two or three volumes.

My illness affected this generous friend. He often came to see me, doing everything he could to distract me.

One day he arrived with a professional tape recorder, a Nagra, and the transcript of what he'd read the night before on the radio. He sat down in front of me and held them out.

"Here, Rania, we're going to play make-believe. You're going to take on my role and I'm going to teach you the tricks of my trade."

In the following days, Abu Sultan shared all the secrets of broadcasting. He taught me to breathe silently, never to arrive at the end of a sentence out of breath, to turn pages without making a noise in front of the microphone, not to wear bracelets or a watch that could make a noise knocking against the table—in short, he taught me how to give a good live performance.

This introduction to radio pleased me enormously and I took to the game even more when Abu Sultan repeated again and again that my voice was good and my diction excellent. I was an assiduous student, which amused and pleased him.

The game soon advanced. Abu Sultan asked me to write my own pieces rather than reading his. I was a little flustered at the prospect.

"Pieces about what?"

"Whatever you like. Describe what you see, write what

goes through your mind. You have no problem doing it in your notebooks."

Taking refuge behind false modesty, I swore that I would never be able to do it. But in fact, as soon as my friend had gone, my pen was scratching the paper furiously as I attacked my first "article." I was ready for our next rendezvous. I had chosen girls' education as my subject.

Abu Sultan adored his role as teacher, but over the course of our meetings I noticed that his tone changed and from paternalism we began to slide toward professionalism, until one evening he declared: "The child has become a woman."

Well, yes! It was high time to acknowledge that. I was after all a mother!

His affection toward me didn't change but our relationship became more adult.

Another evening I was talking to him in his study when the telephone rang. Pretending that he had something urgent to see to, Abu Sultan asked me to pick up the phone and ask the caller to wait. A little surprised, I did it.

In fact, I learned later, my friend had organized a clever trick behind my back. First, without saying anything to me, he had gotten my father to agree to let me work in radio if the opportunity arose. That had not been overly difficult. My father had been very skeptical but in the end had accepted (without, it is true, great enthusiasm) our friend's arguments. That was the first step. And then Abu Sultan had thought of putting me in touch with one of his friends, Mohammed, a scriptwriter who worked for MBC FM, a Saudi station in London. For that, he asked his friend to call at a particular time, knowing that I would be there.

And so there I was talking to Mohammed while Abu Sultan pretended to attend to something else. After several minutes, he took the phone and I heard him reply to his friend, while looking at me with an amused air.

"She's the daughter of one of my friends; she is like my own daughter. Yes, yes, I know, she has a very pretty voice.

And yes, she should certainly do radio, I agree with you, but alas I know her father very well and if you mentioned that to him, he would have a fit!"

I then heard the voice of the stranger crackling in the receiver while my friend's face lit up. His interest roused, and spurred on by the challenge, Mohammed now wanted absolutely to meet me and convince my father. It's so much better when something is prohibited! Which was exactly the scenario that Abu Sultan had envisioned. He knew that the job would be mine because he had lied outrageously: my father had already agreed. It was a perfect strategy! Seated in my armchair, my eyes wide open, I didn't know quite what was afoot.

Abu Sultan hung up and then explained the situation. I couldn't believe my ears. I was happy and thanked him, but at the same time I felt nervous. I wouldn't be able to do it... I was overcome with confusion. Unlike the other Saudi radio stations, which broadcast in classical Arabic, MBC FM was in the language of the street. It was therefore much more popular and had a wider audience. Mohammed was in charge of preparing programs that were much more modern than those traditionally offered on the radio.

He wanted to put an end to the dull material of the past and had thus planned a series on the Egyptian singer Umm Kulthoum, the undisputed star of the Arab world, and all lyricists and arrangers who worked with her. Mohammed wanted to surround himself with a young, dynamic team for these programs. He had just told Abu Sultan that he thought I would fit in well with his staff, if I passed several technical tests.

My mentor didn't waste any time. The very next day, I went to the studios of MBC FM, situated in the center of Jeddah, accompanied by my father. It was out of the question that he would leave me alone among so many men. He had given his agreement, but there were limits.

No sooner had I arrived than I was seated behind a microphone and given a script to read. Mohammed confirmed that he liked my voice, but another man, surly and curt, didn't agree. He hadn't liked my performance and he said so clearly.

"It wasn't any good."

I was furious that my father should witness this failure, for it was clear to me that my radio career was at an end. I was already putting my things away in my bag when Mohammed interrupted, "No, no, Rania, don't leave. We will start again. Radio is a craft; it has to be learned."

I repeated my text ten times over without wearying, enduring the producer's criticisms. Over the following days, I continued my apprenticeship, always accompanied by my father or brother, and with Suleiman, the producer, never sparing me and letting nothing pass. It was horrible. I held on, but I often felt like crying, he was so hard on me. He particularly made me work my voice, continually shouting, "Deeper, deeper, it should come from the guts..."

I made progress nonetheless and soon we began to record the first program of the series. Fourteen others followed. In the end, even Suleiman was satisfied. Laughing, he declared that he had been hard on me to make me get better: "It was for your good; you had to learn quickly!"

Okay. He could still have spared me the slights in front of my father and brother, even if I won out in the end.

The series finished, I again concentrated on my studies, but this experience on the radio had left me curious. It was obvious that the recordings had interested me much more than my lessons. I said nothing to my father, but I sensed a change and that a helping hand from destiny was in the offing.

I learned that one of my neighbors, al-Ammari, was a television director and that he was looking for a female newscaster. I quickly found an excuse to meet him and talk to him about my adventure on MBC FM and my ideas about radio and television.

It all fell wonderfully into place because the channel that employed al-Ammari, Channel 1, also wanted to change its image. The few women who worked there were quite old, austere, and, it had to be said, not very pretty. In addition, many of them were foreigners, like a good number of the male presenters. Channel 1 wanted to have a younger, primarily Saudi broadcast team. My neighbor thought that with the experience I had gained at MBC FM, my application was perfectly natural. He proposed that I should try my hand.

Several days later, I returned to the broadcasting studios for new tests, again accompanied by my father, of course. After radio, I was discovering television.

I followed al-Ammari into a sort of aquarium, a soundproof glass room, and a large metal door closed behind us. It was quite impressive.

Three cameras were in place. Al-Ammari sat me in front of one and held out a book, explaining that a little red light would go on above the camera when the technician began to film.

"Then you read, trying to look into the camera the entire time. It isn't easy."

Several seconds later, a voice came through a loudspeaker: "Five, four, three, two, one, zero." Here we went. I heard the motor of the camera running and I launched in. I felt strangely at ease and had no trouble reading while looking at the camera. It was all going so well that I didn't immediately notice that a red light had lit up on a second camera, and then another on the third. I looked from one to the other according to which light was lit; it was terrifically exciting and I had a feeling that the cameramen were enjoying themselves making me turn my head.

After several minutes, a voice again resounded through the loudspeaker: "It's good—cut."

All smiles, al-Ammari came over to me.

"That was perfect. So good that, as you saw, we used all three cameras. Usually with a beginner we just use one. Well done, you've jumped ahead—that's rare."

And then my neighbor got the tape that we had just recorded and took it away, asking me to wait for him. Several minutes later, he reappeared and announced, "Our director has just viewed your test. He wants to meet with you and your father."

The head of Channel 1, Tarek Riri, was an imposing, courteous, and smiling man. He invited us to sit down, looking at me carefully.

"For a novice, what you did was very good. I want to hire you."

And then, turning to my father, "Do you agree? If Rania worked with us, I would treat her like my own daughter."

Faced with a fait accompli, my father accepted. Tarek Riri then gave me four days to produce my first report.

I cautiously chose to operate in familiar territory and proposed to present the school where I was studying. The principal gave her permission. The cameraman was even given permission to enter the faculty buildings—though on a day, of course, when the students would be absent.

Abu Sultan had prepared for me the questions I should ask as well as the shooting script and the precise editing of the program. I had only to follow his directions. It seemed easy but I was still somewhat nervous.

I met with my principal during the filming, and took advantage of the opportunity to negotiate possible alterations to my study hours, in case my work and classes conflicted. My father had generously, but cautiously, agreed that I should take the television job on the condition that I continued with my schooling. The principal was very accommodating.

This first report went smoothly and others followed. I began to climb the ladder. This progress made me put my illness to the side, even though it was still present. I tried to forget it.

Soon, the management proposed that I should write and present a new program that it wanted to broadcast in the morning: *This Morning in the Kingdom*, a nod to *Good Morning,*

Vietnam. I would present the country warts and all, through reports carried out all over the kingdom.

My investigations allowed me to penetrate our society. I drank in the knowledge I found, and burned my wings on the fire of its contradictions.

My first appearance on television had surprised people, but it didn't provoke the outcry I feared. The privileged classes, who were used to traveling, were not shocked, although it surprised them to see such a bold innovation in Saudi Arabia. The mass of television viewers had been caught short, but didn't know what arguments to make against it. Some people would doubtless have liked to protest but in the name of what? No religious rule had been flouted.

Very quickly I sensed that the public had gotten used to my presence on screen. I was the link between reports and my confidence grew. After several weeks on air, I organized my work myself; I no longer needed Abu Sultan's help. The ratings were steady at first and soon went up—so much that the producers got bolder and increased my workload. I traveled the country in every direction, and most of the time—not always—the authorities received our teams with open arms. I was proud and happy about this for it marked a changing mentality toward women. Our liberation would be slow and difficult, but it was coming. That said, I noticed on the ground that certain sections of the population were resistant. Although I presented myself modestly with my scarf over my head, many men still refused to meet me. I never insisted because it was they who had to take the step of accepting me, not the other way around. I wouldn't force their hand, but would leave them to marginalize themselves.

I also encountered hesitation among women. Some held important posts or were deeply committed to different kinds of work, particularly in the social sector, but would refuse to speak to us. It was not in their customs or tradition to appear on television.

My programs roused more and more interest and I was carried away by this spiraling success. People in positions of local and national power wanted to appear on my program. Those who didn't know about me were consigned to the margins of our culture. Make no mistake: I don't claim that my reports were essential to the life of the kingdom, but they were fashionable and "happening" and it was good to be associated with them, even in a Saudi Arabia so concerned with tradition. It was possible to remain faithful to one's culture without seeing evolution as revolution—that was precisely the educational message that the management of Channel 1 wanted to transmit through me. I was aware that it wasn't always easy to keep a cool head about it. Being both a star and a symbol at 22, in a country in which only men seemed to matter, was quite dizzying. I had to make sure I didn't let it get to me. I had to remain clearheaded; it would be stupid to lose this wonderful experience and fantastic advance for Saudi women.

Thanks to the vigilant help of Abu Sultan and my director, I managed the situation reasonably well, and after several months on the job had been totally embraced by the viewing public, including men, who were watching me in greater and greater numbers. They were getting used to seeing me. My presence onscreen didn't disturb them and some even went as far as saying they liked it. Not only was the notion of a feminine presence on television accepted, but I was headed straight for stardom. Rania, a superstar in Jeddah—that didn't happen every day.

This success brought me freedom. My status as a woman having been accepted, I could now devote myself to my new career as TV journalist, which I found totally absorbing. At every moment of the day I was thinking of possible subjects and looking for new ideas.

One day, I realized that there were no programs marking the anniversary of the declaration of the Kingdom of

Saudi Arabia, the unification of the regions by Ibn Saud on September 23, 1932. It seemed to me that we should commemorate the event and I immediately began working on a project, which I submitted to my director. I envisioned the organization of an official ceremony on a Jeddah beach, with a procession and cavalcade of the Royal Guard in cere- monial dress and then a recreation of the armies of the period in their traditional costumes. The whole thing filmed and broadcast live, if you please! The management staff thought it was a great idea and I was given carte blanche to pull it off.

Alas, over the ensuing days I realized what a hornet's nest I had launched myself into. In principle, there was no problem: everyone applauded, everyone was happy, every- one wanted to take part. But as soon as it was a question of money, organizing rehearsals, or transporting the horses or the men, I came up against mountains of bureaucratic diffi- culties. I did not let this put me off, however.

Stubbornly, I proposed soliciting sponsors for the event, which Saudi Arabia wasn't yet accustomed to. Not only did it work but it brought in money, making my task much easier.

I hung onto the idea of this celebration; I wanted to make it happen and I intended it to be a success. But I still noticed that a lot of the people I spoke to were very surprised to be dealing with a woman. Many who were reluctant ultimately accepted me because I was beginning to have a certain fame, but other doors remained closed.

We managed to overcome all the obstacles and on the evening of September 23rd, when the sun was beginning to go down and the light was softest, we gave our viewers the first big televised parade of our history.

For over an hour, the cavaliers' cloaks flapped in the wind to the rhythm of the gallop of their broad-backed, muscular Arab horses. Regimental music burst out from all over the beach, blending with the shouts of an enthusiastic crowd. It was a real joy to see all these people delighted by the spectacle. The program was a big hit and my popularity increased still further.

This fame did not give me dispensation from my duties as a Muslim woman or from patriarchal customs. Being single—my new status obliterated the fact of my divorce—I had many suitors. Men, and not insignificant ones, again asked my father for my hand in marriage, and he didn't hesitate to sift selectively through the candidates. It was crazy! Incidentally, my father no longer lamented the sight of his daughter on television; he was almost happy with it. One more means by which to affirm his paternal authority and rights.

I was willing to let him manage my marital future as he chose as long as he didn't impose a husband on me; when it came to it, I fully intended to exercise my right to have a say in the matter. I was no longer a little girl and while I willingly submitted to the laws of the Qur'an, which I respected, there are social errors that we should not be forced to repeat.

For the time being, I had other preoccupations besides looking for a husband. Television took up my time, I still went regularly to the university, and my little free time was devoted to my daughter Rahaf. I didn't see where a man would fit into all that.

But the suitors became more and more pressing and came from all sides. One day, in the corridors of the television studios, one of them made an enflamed declaration to me. He was a singer in his forties with olive skin who had come to record a song for a variety program; he had rushed from the recording studio to come and talk to me when he saw me passing in the corridor. He overwhelmed me with compliments, swearing that I was the ideal woman he dreamed of, praising the quality of my programs and the talent with which I presented them. A whirlwind of praises, before the grand announcement that he planned to ask my father for my hand in marriage; he already knew his address.

It all happened so quickly that I was incapable of saying anything in reply. I stammered something banal and left him to his fantasies. When I got back to my office I nonetheless asked who the man was.

"Rachid," I was told, "a singer of African origin. He doesn't stop asking questions about you."

A singer... of African origin... I imagined my father's expression if Rachid turned up to ask for my hand. After a daughter on television, such a son-in-law! For someone who had once thought only of oil, finance, and the economy, he was going to get a shock.

Married Again

Several days after our first meeting in a corridor of Channel 1, Rachid did indeed go to see my poor father and ask for my hand. My father almost choked. A singer! An African! That was all he needed. For the Saudi middle classes, Africans are still thought of as servants. Everyone, they believe, should know their station; one didn't mix with them.

At first my father refused outright. But Rachid persisted, harassing my father and taking no notice of his refusals. For my part I no longer viewed the idea so negatively. The extravagance and nerve of this tall and seductive man amused me. I found him attractive. He found more opportunities to run into me and no day passed when I did not see him. He lay siege to my office and, as soon as he saw me, launched into grandiloquent and impassioned declarations. Rachid's excesses made me curious to see how far he would go. I even got to the point of wanting him to appear; I was flattered by his determination to win my hand. I said as much to my father, who wasn't surprised. He now expected anything from me, but for him, this was too much. I drove him to despair.

Particularly because Rachid gave my father no respite, but continually barraged him. He frankly spied on him, followed him around all day, and went up to him whenever he could to plead his case. My father even began to think that I was lying to him and that I was already in a relationship with this man. He told me of his doubts. This suspicion annoyed me; the next time I saw Rachid, I asked him to stop bothering my father. I criticized his approach because it irritated my father, but at the same time I admired the singer's constancy and doggedness. Father was much less enthusiastic and he soon exploded: "I gave you your freedom by accepting that you work on television and here is my thanks. Because of this, we'll put an end to reports and studios. From now on, you stay at home."

With these words he shut me in my room and called my director to say I was ill. I was kept in the house for two months.

Rachid still didn't give up. He told one of his sisters, who lived in the United States, of the situation and asked for her help. The young woman immediately rushed to Jeddah and asked to meet my father. Bending the rules, my father agreed to discuss the matter with a woman. Because she lived in America. That was the way it was. Not only did he see her but she managed to change his mind.

My father entered my room brusquely, a bundle of banknotes in his hand.

"Do you really want to marry this Rachid?"

Caught off guard, I threw myself into the water: "Yes."

With a curt gesture, my father threw the money on my bed.

"Very well—here is your dowry."

Against all expectations, he had given in. His attitude had changed overnight. If I wanted to marry an African entertainer, I should go ahead and do it; after all, it was my business and from now on he washed his hands of it. He gave his agreement but on the condition that it be over and done with as quickly as possible and my situation stabilized. In exchange for his authorization, he made just one demand of Rachid: he could sing as much as he wanted in the evening, but he should find an "honest" job during the day.

Overjoyed at having got what he wanted, my transfixed admirer gave himself over to the search for a steady job, but quickly realized that he had no leads and even fewer skills. One of his friends nonetheless unearthed a vague administrative job in the Jeddah chamber of commerce. That would do. Honor would be saved.

Thus provided for, Rachid had the green light to marry me. I said nothing but I couldn't imagine him in his new job. I couldn't see him sitting behind a desk dealing with red tape all day. We would see. In any case, there were now no obstacles to my marriage. I had no idea that I was heading straight for disaster. My destiny was being played out and my life was about to start crumbling into pieces...

My second wedding was nothing like the first. There was no question of a big celebration; this time the preparations were dealt with swiftly and with the utmost discretion. Without announcement or invitations, the ceremony was over in a few minutes. It was limited to a purely judicial act. My father seemed impatient to have the whole thing over with and he wasn't even concerned when he found out that Rachid didn't have a cent to his name. That didn't interest him; he only wanted me to disappear from his house and even his life. He said this to me clearly: once the union was formalized, he didn't want to see me anymore. I would no longer exist for him. My father found this marriage to a man of African origin very hard to take. Saudi society, particularly the middle classes, is still very hesitant about mixed marriages. My father didn't oppose the marriage outright because he was relieved to see me go. The other members of the family were hardly more enthusiastic at the idea of an African joining the family; even my uncle Farid conveyed this. No one wanted to celebrate. I then found myself quickly excluded from the circle of their friends.

Since the marriage was pulled off at the speed of light, I didn't have time to think about how my life would change. As soon as I began to glimpse that the changes would not be for the better, I had already committed to a life with Rachid.

I quickly realized that his artistic career was an illusion. He didn't have a single engagement or contract in the offing, and no plans. Other surprises awaited me. My new husband confided at the last moment that he was divorced. I hadn't known. He already had three girls and a boy, two of whom would come to live with us. I was faced with a fait accompli. I didn't like this last-minute revelation or the fact that the children were being imposed on me without my opinion being asked, but I couldn't withdraw. Or more precisely, I didn't want to withdraw. Already, there had been too many complications in my life. I accepted out of weariness, not knowing what a mess I was getting into.

It was only after the move into my new accommodation with Rahaf, Rachid, and his children that I finally understood my situation. Having known my grandfather's vast family house in Mecca as a child, finding myself in the tiny two-room apartment that Rachid had taken in the building where his parents lived was hard to accept. Obviously times had changed and the size of modern apartments was different from that of the homes of the past, but I felt shut in with our few square meters of space. The transition was too rapid. The furniture went with the place: a Formica table, four non-matching chairs, a large bed covered with a mattress as hard as wood, and that was about it. For cooking I had to make do with rusty and battered kitchen utensils.

I didn't have the time to feel sorry for myself because, fortunately, I had planned a magnificent honeymoon. I needed a change of scenery. Thanks to my television work, I had saved up some money, which I would spend with my husband in London and Paris. My parents would look after Rahaf and Rachid's children would return to their mother during our adventure. After all the upheaval in my life, a special trip seemed as though it would do me some good. In several months, my life had been turned completely upside down and I wanted to pause and catch my breath again.

I already knew London because I had been there with my parents when my father had gone on business, and I was impatient to rediscover a city I had loved. Above all, I was keen to show it to my husband. But Rachid did not share my enthusiasm. During the flight he asked me no questions about England; he was concerned only with the hotel where we would be staying. I had reserved a room in the Sheraton in the center of town, which seemed to suit him, but he didn't want to know anything else. Such lack of interest in our trip astonished me, but at first I put it down to emotion.

I realized, from the moment we got to the hotel, that I was completely wrong. As soon as we were settled in our room, Rachid collapsed into an armchair in front of the television, while I put his clothes away in the closet. I said nothing. I ran a bath and, without worrying myself further about my husband, slid into the warm water to relax.

Half an hour later, Rachid had hardly moved an inch. He had helped himself to a fruit juice, which he sipped in his armchair, his eyes half-closed. I opened the curtains. Outside, London was pulsating with noise and life. I had a wild desire to go and lose myself in the crowd. Turning to Rachid, I asked him, "Do you want to take a bath before going out?"

"No. I don't want to go out."

It was barely noon. I looked at him, dumbfounded. "We're not going to stay here the whole day?"

"Yes, why not? We're fine here."

Three days. We stayed inside for three days without putting a foot outside; three days locked in the hotel. Breakfast in the room, lunch in the restaurant below, and dinner in the restaurant above. And it was forbidden to go out alone: it was the husband who gave the orders. It was grim.

After three days of virtual imprisonment, I thought the joke had lasted long enough. I hadn't come on honeymoon to London to watch television in a room and make love. Exasperated, I had a last try with Rachid.

"You still don't want to go out?"

"I've told you no; this room suits me perfectly."

"Then I'm going out by myself!"

Rachid jumped from his armchair: "What?"

"You heard me: I'm going out by myself. It's beautiful out, we're in London and I'm not going to stay enclosed in these four walls for my whole trip."

"If you go out, I'll kill you."

Regardless, I put on a jacket and then pretended to go out by slamming the door of the room; in fact, I waited next to the door to see his reaction. I heard the sound of a great upheaval. Amused, I waited. Several seconds later my husband came rushing by a demon; in his hurry, he knocked into me. Seeing I had not gone out, he calmed down and said, "Okay, I'll come with you."

I took him to Hyde Park and then we took a taxi to Piccadilly, with Rachid never saying a word or showing any interest in anything. He sulked liked a child, until in the end I wasn't unhappy to go back to the hotel. The next day, without asking his advice, I told him I was going out by myself. He grumbled a bit but accepted it.

I finally took advantage of the city and had fun getting lost in it, spending hours browsing in all the departments of the famous Harrods; I even treated myself to watching the changing of the guard at Buckingham Palace. How could Rachid pass up all this? I couldn't understand.

For my part I wanted to have fun and get as much as I could out of this vacation, so I decided on the ultimate folly: to go out in a miniskirt. Yes, a miniskirt—unthinkable in Saudi Arabia! I knew that Allah forbid it but I promised him that I would only do it once, just one little time to try it out. I told Rachid of my plan, because I needed his permission.

He was outraged and acted as if I were insane.

"In a miniskirt? Really short? People will see your thighs? Don't even think of it."

But yes, I had already thought of just that. And I had expected his reaction. As luck would have it, several minutes later in the hotel elevator a Spanish tourist took a long look at me, and said to Rachid, "Congratulations. You have a very sexy wife."

What a disaster! I expected the worst and anxiously waited for my husband's reaction. There was no doubt he was going to knock this lout flat... To my enormous surprise, Rachid smiled, accepted the compliment, even seemed flattered by it, and offered a casual, "Thank you."

But as soon as the Spanish tourist left the elevator the judgment came my way: "He finds you sexy when you're dressed normally. Can you imagine what it would be like in a miniskirt?"

That didn't stop me wanting to try it. It was God who resolved the problem: it wasn't very warm in London and on top of that it was raining. It simply wasn't miniskirt weather. Exit the fantasy.

During our whole stay, Rachid only went out three times, one of which was a memorable trip to the cinema. Again I didn't manage to get a word out of him—not a single word or comment, either on London or the film. On leaving the cinema, I suddenly broke down in tears and sat down on the edge of the pavement. Irrepressible sobs shook me and—something rare in London, where nobody attracts attention—intrigued passers-by began to gather and form a circle around us. Seeing this, Rachid panicked, looked desperately around him, seized me brusquely in his arms, and hurled me over his shoulders like a sack of potatoes. Then he left with huge strides, desperately looking for a taxi. When he finally found one he threw me inside and pulled the door sharply behind him, as if he wanted to escape from the crowd. Finally he breathed and relaxed.

I also felt better and apologized. When we realized what we had just done, we burst out laughing.

The following day I took to my solitary walks again, leaving, without regret, my husband in front of his television screen. When I got back, I found a surprise: Rachid had gone. Not a note or a message at the desk. I went to the bar, the restaurants, the shops: he wasn't there... It was amazing. I wondered what it was that could suddenly have taken him outside. A mystery.

Rachid got back to the hotel just after 6PM. I immediately questioned him.

"What's going on? Why didn't you tell me you wanted to go out? Where were you?"

"I had an appointment with someone in television to discuss a contract."

I was thunderstruck. We had been in England for a good ten days and my husband had never spoken of this mysterious contract. It was a bit much. I demanded to know more: "What contract?"

"A variety show, with songs, for a channel that broadcasts in Arabic. But I don't think it will work out."

"You could have told me about it—I would have come with you."

"Exactly. I didn't want that. I know you. You would have played your game and stolen my thunder by proposing an idea of your own. No question."

I was flabbergasted by this reply. My own husband was suspicious of me; he hid things from me because he was afraid I would take his place... What trust that seemed to promise! His attitude disturbed and disappointed me very much. I told him this, reminding him that I was a wife and a Muslim and that for those two reasons I would never do anything that could harm him. Rachid listened to me but didn't seem convinced. That hurt me.

After this fruitless outing, my husband didn't leave the room again until our departure. The failure of his professional proposal had made him even more despondent. Where was the lively, dynamic man who had courted me?

After London, I had planned a stopover of five days in Paris. The City of Light would perhaps cheer my husband up. I hoped, but I no longer really believed. He had asked no more questions about France than he had about England. It was a bad sign.

Arriving in Paris, I did my accounts and realized that I would have to tighten my purse strings. My funds were not inexhaustible and I would have to watch over Rachid's caprices and desire for luxury.

Our hotel, less grand than the one in London, was nonetheless situated a stone's throw from the Champs-Élysées. That the room was less spacious than the one in the Sheraton was paradoxically a plus: Rachid was less happy in it, and so immediately agreed to accompany me on a long walk from the Arc de Triomphe to the Concorde. To say he was transported with joy would be an exaggeration, but it was still progress because in London he hadn't even seen the Marble Arch. Nonetheless, over the next days I got angry because I couldn't get him to go further than the Champs-Élysées. I spoke to him in vain about the Opera, Montmartre, Montparnasse—he didn't want to know about anything. Even the Eiffel Tower didn't interest him. For five days we scoured the shops and cafés in our immediate area. I found it frustrating but I no longer had the heart to go off by myself. Rachid had deigned to leave the room and that was at least something. I couldn't let him wander like a lost soul around the streets bordering our hotel. So I sacrificed myself, but with the firm intention of coming back to Paris in other circumstances to explore the city to my heart's content.

In short, my honeymoon didn't leave me with unforgettable memories.

Back in Jeddah, my heart was heavy. Not only had Rachid spoiled my trip to Europe but he hadn't uttered a word of thanks, when I had treated him like a king. It was almost I who had to thank him for the time he had kindly given me. Without mentioning his secret little television appointment, which still stuck in my throat.

He was not bothered by any of it. Everything seemed natural to him—as natural as the tiny flat in which he forced us to live. His work was his only preoccupation. Not because he was passionate about it but, the exact opposite, because it bored him. As I had thought, my husband couldn't bear having to go to an office every morning. For him it was torture and an affront to his artistic vocation. Every evening I would hear him moaning and lamenting his lot, without ever asking me if I was all right or needed help. And yet I expended vast resources of energy and ingenuity in making our apartment pleasant, spending a large part of my television salary on furniture or decorations. I played with colors and shapes to enlarge the space and brighten it as much as possible, but it wasn't easy.

Rachid saw nothing and said nothing. Never a compliment or a kind word. Never a cent either—this didn't even seem to cross his mind and he never spoke of it. My husband must have thought his salary so miserable that it would be indecent for me to expect him to chip in to family expenses. Therefore I made do with what I had to support the entire family.

The burden finally became so heavy that one morning, after four months of this regime, I threw in the towel. Everything came into my mind and got mixed up: London, Paris, my physical and financial efforts, the lack of recognition... I'd had enough and I announced to Rachid that I was leaving with Rahaf to go to my uncle Farid, whom I had not seen since my marriage. For even my uncle and aunt, whom I loved so much and who loved me so much, had cold-shouldered me since I had married Rachid. My husband's Sudanese origins did not go over well and even the two people whom I appreciated most in the world couldn't manage to disregard them. They had withdrawn from me; that they'd accepted to put me up with my daughter meant only that they saw the beginnings of a separation. Everything that distanced me from Rachid brought me closer to them.

After a week at my uncle's, Rachid arrived, contrite and repentant. He gave me a necklace as a peace offering and begged me to come back to live with him, swearing that he loved me more than anything and could not live without me. I was weak enough to believe him. I still hesitated, but my uncle, in an effort to make peace, also advised me to go back to my apartment, even if it was hard for him to see me leave again with this man he didn't like.

For a few days, my husband was attentive. I was also in a good mood and I decided to take the opportunity to make peace by making a fuss of my husband. I even rigged up a sort of Moroccan sauna for him with a little gas bottle installed in the bathroom to make the steam. Rachid was very pleased with this arrangement until a technical hitch occurred: he was sprayed with a jet of burning water that turned him into a lobster. He was hurt but still, we couldn't help laughing.

To make up for it, I offered to massage him and, bingo, I made things worse by tearing off bits of well-cooked skin. But Rachid was in a good mood, for despite that we again collapsed with laughter.

The lull did not last. He soon became jealous and aggressive again, calling me ten times a day from his office to keep tabs on me. He exploded with rage when he knew I was on television or working on a report.

"There are too many men there; it can't go on," he continually repeated.

My only defense consisted of pointing out to him that if I didn't work, I didn't know how we would eat. He still didn't give me a penny of his salary, which angered me more and more because I had discovered that he regularly gave a bit of money to his parents. I had the unpleasant feeling that I was supporting the entire family and that upset me.

I nonetheless forced myself to respect the rules that I had set for myself in the name of my religion. I ensured that our apartment was always impeccable and pleasant to live in, despite its minuscule size, and every day I cooked the little dishes that everyone admired so much. Even Rachid acknowledged my talent as a cook and would comment on it to the rare guests he invited to the house. An exceptional compliment on his part! All my women friends admired the efforts I made to assume my role as mistress of the house as best I could.

Between my house and Channel 1 there was precious little time left for the university and the inevitable happened: one morning I received a letter telling me I had been expelled for lack of attendance. To tell the truth, this didn't sadden me. I had given up on radiology a long time ago. And another issue preoccupied me: I was pregnant. I love children and so in principle it was good news, but I wondered how we were all going to live in a two-room apartment. It seemed impossible, as did the question of how I could keep working as my pregnancy progressed.

Rachid rapidly resolved this last point, but in the worst way, in a completely irresponsible manner. His irascible temperament took over and he became more and more jealous, not only of men but of women too—indeed, of anyone who came near me. He said it clearly: my place was in the house and that was all there was to it. He couldn't tolerate my television work and he wanted me to give it up. This idea became his obsession.

It was during this period that he forbade me from receiving or making phone calls. One evening when a friend from Channel 1 called me for the first time, my husband went even further: he rushed over, wrenched the telephone from my hands and slapped me violently. It was the beginning of the journey that would take us to hell.

The violence of the blow threw me against the wall. I was dizzy and stunned. It was the first time Rachid had hit me. I couldn't believe he would do that, particularly when I was pregnant. Frightened, I ran to take refuge in my room, where I doubled-locked the door.

The next day, I was sporting a fine black eye. I felt ashamed and told everyone who asked me that I had walked into a door. As for Rachid, he didn't back down; he had no regrets about what he had done. Not a word of apology. On the contrary, he didn't stop demanding that I leave television. His older brother came to reason with him. He knew that Rachid had hit me and reproached him but it didn't do any good. My husband didn't change his tune: my future was in the home and nowhere else. My brother-in-law begged me not to leave and to be patient. I'd had enough. I was tired of it all and I threw in the towel: my husband won. So that he wouldn't hit me again, I left Channel 1 on the excuse that my pregnancy was forcing me to stop. I nonetheless assured my director that I would take up my post again as soon as I could. It would hurt me too much to tell him that I was giving up forever. A whole aspect of my life was crumbling away. The central driving force in my life, the only force that truly helped me go on had just disappeared. I didn't have the courage to confront it and yet I knew that the decision was suicidal.

Not long afterward, a friend, Khadija, a radio presenter, called me.

"Is it true what they're saying? You're leaving television?"

"Yes. Rachid is causing too many problems. I had to find a solution and I've given up; I don't want a second divorce."

"Rania, you know you're making a mistake, you can't do that. You should talk to your father about it."

"That would only complicate things. My decision is irrevocable. You've chosen your career and I've chosen my home."

After I hung up, I collapsed into an chair. I hoped that Rachid would one day realize the enormity of the sacrifice I had just made for him. Yet I doubted it; I had a feeling that he wanted to destroy me and that was all he cared about.

I gave birth to our first son, Saoud, and we moved into a bigger apartment, with four rooms. It wasn't luxurious but it was more comfortable. It wasn't enough to lift my spirits, however. For weeks I remained stuck inside my four walls, with only my sofa for a friend. Only it knew my despair. We shared our long hours of solitude and the same agony: I was slowly fading away on its cushions, which sagged under my weight as time went on. We were destroying each other.

I needed a solution to get out of the impasse in which I found myself and the boredom that was gnawing away at me.

A crazy idea suddenly came to me. Our sitting room was big enough; during the day I could turn it into a make-up parlor. I wasn't a beautician but I had gotten used to make-up when I worked in television and I had often made up my friends and sisters, who had always appreciated my efforts.

I immediately got hold of four chairs and two small tables and sketched out the design of my new world. There was no big investment or charges involved—the idea was marvelous. That evening, I presented it to Rachid, trying to lure him with the possible benefits. He agreed immediately, for he saw nothing but advantages in the project. Aside from the not insignificant financial aspect, I would be obliged to stay at home, where I would receive only women—a model wife. My proposal conformed perfectly to Rachid's idea of a married couple. He had succeeded in shutting me away and was happy.

I was much less so. Materially, my solution was a good one. Morally it was something else. Thanks to word of mouth, I soon had a reasonable clientele, but this new occupation didn't make me forget the old one. I missed television.

And to cap it all off, my new situation opened my eyes to certain anomalies in my husband's life.

When I worked outside the house, I couldn't control his comings and goings and in any case didn't dream of doing so—I had too much of my own work to do. But when I was confined to the house I realized that he was often absent. His behavior aroused my curiosity and some suspicions. He was totally uninterested in his family, often went out at night, and I was soon convinced that he had a mistress, or even several. In fact he did not love me; he demanded only that I be his possession and now that he had got what he wanted, he could cheerfully devote himself to other women.

I wanted to be sure of this, however, and one day when Rachid was preparing to leave the house, without offering me any explanation, I asked him, "Where are you going?"

Surprised that I dared ask him his business, his expression tightened and he tried to get out of answering with evasions that did not satisfy me. I wanted to know exactly what he was hiding from me and I didn't let go. Little used to such resistance, my husband lost his footing and eventually admitted that he was indeed having an affair.

What a shock! I had to sit down to take it in. Bigamy is frequent and allowed in Saudi Arabia but I would have liked to have known that I had competition. It was unpleasant to discover it after two years of marriage. His secret exposed, Rachid tried to justify himself.

"I swear, I'll break it off."

"You can do whatever you want. I want a divorce."

Yes, in that moment I wanted it, but the specter of another shameful separation paralyzed me. A divorce is already badly viewed in Saudi Arabia—as for two! That was what held me back. Despite everything, I continued to explore my husband's life, which still held quite a few surprises. The revelation of this affair encouraged me to begin looking more closely at Rachid's activities. A rapid enquiry of his friends and of shopkeepers, a closer monitoring of his timetables, and some cross-checking of his contradictions soon proved to me that his life was full of other women whom he had not told me about. Now that I was vigilant, certain details left no doubt: my husband had many mistresses. But what to do about it?

Unfortunately, while I was coming to these realizations, a much more serious problem loomed. My husband left his job. How were we going to live? We weren't going to get far with the meager resources I cobbled together by making up my friends. It was perfect as a little extra but insufficient to support a whole family.

This time, Rachid would have to stir himself to find another job and contribute to the family budget. I had long since given up the illusion that his songs would bring in any money; he was the only one who believed in his talent. We had no options left and I presented him with the reality. We needed solutions. This ultimatum angered him but I didn't care. Several days later, he set out a project that seemed to me at first completely surreal and ridiculous: to earn money he would sell used cars. But only big-engined European and American cars such as Mercedes, Audis, or Cadillacs. All these cars are very expensive in Saudi Arabia and the secondhand market barely existed. Rachid therefore proposed to take orders and then to buy the cars in Germany or the United States. He had looked at the figures and calculated his profit margins and he thought it could work. I didn't have much confidence in it, but why not, after all? At least he was trying something. And while he was traveling I could live a little and see my friends in peace. Or so I thought.

Shortly afterward, Rachid left for the port of Hamburg with several firm orders. His clients had made their choices, fixed on a price, and paid in advance. He made his purchases abroad and then loaded the vehicles onto a cargo ship headed for Jeddah, where the new owners would come to collect them. He then flew back to Saudi Arabia. To my great surprise, the system worked, which relieved me considerably.

It was time that I had some good news because new misfortunes had befallen me, as if I didn't have enough already. I was suddenly afflicted with violent headaches. The painkillers I took made no difference and I had to consult my doctor. My condition was serious and had only gotten worse since my first epileptic fits. I would have to undergo a fairly serious and risky operation. My spirits dipped again.

In fact, the doctors planned three operations. They went smoothly and the surgeons even announced that they had found the cause of my epilepsy and had been able to correct it. I would no longer be tortured by this illness. It was marvelous news that turned out to be true.

Rachid barely came to see me during my stay in hospital—just two or three hasty visits. I wasn't even sad about it; I was beyond that.

Yet we were still a couple, as was confirmed by the news that I was pregnant once more. An accident. I didn't want to have another child but Allah forbade me from withdrawing from my conjugal duties and the precautions to which I had access were not enough. All I can say is that the prospect of being a mother again only made my burden heavier.

I had the impression that the best years of my life were slipping between my fingers. My youth was drying up before my eyes and I was shriveling up like an ancient mummy.

Imprisoned in my apartment, I was totally cut off from the world. I never went out, even with my husband. We couldn't go out because we didn't have the money to buy a car. I had to resign myself to watching the women that Rachid invited for his clients parade before my eyes, while I was forbidden from going out.

I adapted myself to this life until I gave birth. My son's delivery had been difficult and this was even worse. When

I gave birth to my second boy, Nayef, I hemorrhaged, and the surgeons had to make an emergency intervention. I just survived but had to stay in the hospital for two long months.

My husband was no more interested in our second son than in the first. As for my health, it was the least of his worries—he never once asked about it. His visits could be counted on the fingers of one hand. Fortunately my mother and beloved aunt were taking care of me. My aunt particularly took things in hand, transforming my room into a glorious chaos of flowers, trinkets, and photos. It was still not lively enough for her taste and she showed up one day with a bird cage!

It was a strange stay, split between laughter and tears. The nurses thought that I was cheerful, always joking and in a good mood. They would often come to visit, asking me about my past television career and congratulating me on my performances. Their company warmed my heart and chased away my boredom. But these women did not realize that often when they left I would cry like a child, without any particular reason, just because I felt unhappy and terribly alone. The nights seemed endless. I couldn't sleep. I tossed and turned in my bed, black thoughts mingling in my mind. One day I told my aunt about my insomnia and she immediately blamed the birds. According to her, their incessant chirruping kept me from sleeping. The poor canaries had nothing to do with it (from sunset onward they remained perfectly quiet) but it didn't make any difference—my aunt had made her mind up and, bang, away went the cage. I didn't sleep any better but I didn't dare tell my dear aunt.

When I went back to my house after this long stay in the hospital, I had the unpleasant surprise of learning that in my absence, the two other children from Rachid's first marriage had gotten into the habit of staying in our house. I disliked this intrusion of the two young girls, particularly because I found the house in an unspeakable mess. My daughter told me that whenever they visited, my husband's children delighted in destroying everything in the house. Despite my protestations Rachid didn't stop having them over and I had to put up with them more and more often. It was a trial because these little demons did all they could to upset me and annoy Rahaf. One day, for example, I found that my fruit juice had a strange taste. It hadn't passed the sell-by date and I couldn't understand where this bitterness could have come from. Rahaf then confided that she had seen Rachid's children pouring some product into the bottle. That had gone too far—they might have poisoned us. I alerted my husband and demanded that he put an end to such goings-on. Several minutes later, he gathered his little family around him but issued no remonstration. On the contrary, he smiled at his children, who soon returned to their destructive games. Without the least embarrassment, my husband explained that they were naughty with me because I had taken their daddy from them and that since then their mother had been unhappy. I should try to understand them...

It was too much! Rachid had moved heaven and earth to marry me, all the while keeping from me the fact that he was already married—and now I had to accept his children's revenge because I had stolen their father! I was outraged. My patience had limits; my life was a complete hell, and I sensed that I was going to crack.

To calm myself, I reflected on my situation, and decided that I would visit Mecca. I needed to see things more clearly and I hoped that Allah would help me do this. Several days later I entrusted my children to my aunt and left for the Holy City. Rachid didn't dare oppose this religious act.

This break brought me peace. Walking around the Black Stone meditating, I tapped new forces. And I decided to put the pieces back together once again with Rachid, but to define my territory better and impose my norms on him.

When I returned, I told my husband of my intentions, ordering him first of all to put an end to his children's visits. He grumbled but accepted. A turn of events gave Rachid the excuse he needed to give the little girls back: we had to move again, which would disturb our daily lives for some time.

Our landlord wanted his property back and we had to vacate our apartment. It wasn't planned, but we had no choice and I again went in search of a new place, which I found quite quickly.

Our new home, with a floor tiled in white marble, was light and spacious. It was a good deal, but I hoped that Rachid would continue with his car business in Germany and the United States—if not, we would have money worries. This was a sinister premonition, for these problems did not take long in coming.

On September 11, 2001, a special newsflash interrupted television programs all over the world and the images that would remain engraved forever in the memory of history and humanity appeared on the screen: airplanes crashing into the Twin Towers in Manhattan, the most insane act of terrorism ever committed. Bin Laden, the founder of al-Qaeda, a Saudi Arabian who had been stripped of his citizenship, was at the origin of the operation.

In the ensuing hours, a wind of madness blew over the planet. All the Western countries condemned this barbarous act and those responsible for it, while certain Arab countries rejoiced, officially or not, in the terrible blow to New York, the heart of the US. Commentators immediately pointed to Saudi Arabia, accusing it of having long encouraged terror-ism and of training suicide bombers. Everywhere, people suspected Saudi Arabians. They were refused entry visas, their passports were scrutinized in airports, questions were asked about their destinations and reasons for travel. Soon, every foreign trip became a headache for us with the permanent risk that we would be turned away at a border without explanation. Rachid didn't escape this rule. With his frequent trips to the United States and Germany for ill-defined commercial reasons, he was an ideal target for suspicion. Very soon he announced that his work was no longer possible: "I'm giving up. The Americans won't give me a visa and the Germans are just waiting for an opportunity to throw me in prison because they're convinced my cars are just a cover for other activities."

There was nothing to say to this. It did indeed seem impossible to continue. But how were we going to live? Rachid had no other work and it was vital I find a solution. Quickly!

I had to go back to television and even to university. Rachid had ruined my life enough and had taken advantage of me for years; now it was time for me to wake up. He would have to accept it. I'd had enough of being miserable and of his sick and unjustified jealousy. In any case, my husband had nothing else to propose. He was even surprised to hear a woman talking about her plans for the future—for him, it was completely new. However that may be, it was obvious that only television could get us out of the mess we were in. And I really liked the idea of going back before the cameras. I'd had enough of a hard time.

The die was cast: I would return to Channel 1.

A Woman in Saudi Arabia

Despite my three years absence from Channel 1, Tarek Riri gave me a warm reception. What a relief! I had feared that my director might have changed his plans while I was away or even found a replacement for me. These doubts raced through my head while I was waiting on the phone, but as soon as the secretary put me through to my boss, I was reassured.

"Rania, how lovely to hear from you! How are you? When are you coming back?"

My fears disappeared with his words. I immediately replied: "That was precisely why I was calling you. I'd like to take back my post. If you agree..."

"But of course, with great pleasure! When can you come and see us?"

I didn't dare say "at once," even though those words were burning on the tip of my tongue. Prudently, I let Tarek choose a date. I met him three days later. In several minutes everything was sorted out and I had signed a new contract.

My return to the office was very emotional for me. I gazed at it for a long time, breathing deeply; I was back in the right place. I had lost enough time and didn't want Rachid to keep me at the bottom of my profession. Subjects for reports filled my head and I launched into the first immediately. It was time to give my life a good clearing out.

The first thing I did was to re-enroll at the university, this time to study sociology, a subject that would be useful to me in my work. It would facilitate my interviews and help me understand situations better. I felt that choosing this new direction was a significant step, proof that my return to television was definitive. It was a commitment rather than an interlude.

In my private life, I also made two big decisions. First, I asked Rachid to entrust his son and daughter to their mother, for I no longer had the time or the desire to look after them.

Second, I wanted to be closer to my family, whom I didn't see as much as I would like. I didn't want Rachid's diktats anymore. He resisted but I didn't give in.

"You have been poisoning my life for seven years and I've had enough. If you don't like it, if you keep me from going back to television or seeing my family or friends, I'm divorcing you. You won't see me anymore."

I didn't have the time to say "anymore": Rachid hit me violently. This time, I didn't lose a second. I rushed to the telephone and called my parents; my brother picked up. I asked him to come and get me and shut myself in my room to pack my bags.

When I got to my parents', with my children, I breathed deeply and experienced a marvelous moment of freedom. I felt as though I were waking up from a nightmare and I swore that I would never again leave this place. My father welcomed me, worried. He didn't yet know why I was turning up like this at his house, without warning, with my belongings. I got straight to the point.

"I've left Rachid."

My father was stunned. I explained what had just happened and I feared his reaction, but to my great surprise, he gave me a big smile.

"Make yourself at home. It's the best day of my life."

I really wanted to reply that it was also the best day of my life, but he didn't give me time; he turned away and left me to my mother. I realized later that my father wasn't thinking of my happiness. He was simply relieved that I wasn't living with an African anymore. My mother ran from the other end of the apartment. My brother had told her the news.

"My poor girl. Rachid hasn't improved?"

"Oh no! It gets worse and worse."

"So divorce."

"I'm thinking about it."

Three months elapsed during which my husband besieged the house. As he had when he'd wanted to marry me, he pursued my father, begging him to convince me to go back and promising to be the kindest of husbands. To avoid this pressure, my father suggested that I should go back. I refused, until I caught sight of Rachid in the street. He had neglected himself and his clothes were in a mess. It was painful to see. It was my turn to give in and I agreed to go back to the marital home. But on one condition: that my husband leave me alone and let me live as I saw fit.

And so I decided to accept my destiny again and to set things straight. I'd had enough of my husband's riotous lifestyle, but I'd decided to live with him again and would commit myself to it fully, without complaint, letting go of the fact that Rachid had no more income and taking on the financial burden cheerfully and willingly.

Over the next few months we experienced a period of calm. I began to think that my husband had finally settled down. It was an illusion. Bit by bit, his faults rose to the surface again, his aggression reappeared and one day voices were raised, insults given, and it began all over again. Rachid hit me in the face. Luckily I saw the blow coming and managed to soften it, then immediately took refuge in my room.

Over the next few days, the atmosphere became poisonous again. Our arguments became more and more frequent. The blows, too. Rachid blamed me for my fame. He no longer dared ask me to leave my job, because my salary constituted our sole source of income, but he was furious at being stuck playing second fiddle, and he picked fights at the slightest opportunity. I stood up to him and didn't give in. It was during this period that I dreamed of my own death and wrote my will.

Unable to forbid me from working in television for the obvious financial reasons, Rachid kept me on a tight leash, controlling my hours and movements, demanding that I outline my schedule to him. He forbade me from seeing anyone outside my working hours and soon I couldn't even call my friends in front of him. I tried again to be patient and understanding in order to save our relationship but the situation was becoming unbearable and Rachid's obsessive jealousy seemed truly insane. He frightened me.

My fears were justified. Argument after argument, and then came that terrible April 4, 2004, when, for a simple telephone call and a few words exchanged with a woman friend, he beat me savagely, destroying my face and disfiguring me, before leaving me for dead in front of a hospital.

Because our society has had enough of these practices from another age, the images of this dramatic act of aggression were distributed throughout the whole world. The simple news story took on a symbolic value; politicians seized hold of it and it became an affair of state, making me the ambassador of Saudi women. I wasn't expecting this role, and at first it terrified me. I saw in it a dangerous confusion of objectives and was afraid that I was being used to condemn

Saudi Arabia, denounce our political regime and its leaders, a role I refused. I don't want international condemnation to be concentrated on our country.

It is not the condition of women in Saudi Arabia specifically that must be denounced, but that of all the women in the world who suffer under such subjugation. My country must not become the scapegoat for the whole Muslim community: that would be too easy! And Rachid's act must, despite everything, be placed in its rightful context: my husband was psychotically jealous. These two aspects are for me of primary importance. I mustn't mistake my field of combat: I demand justice and not vengeance.

My attitude toward Rachid after my attack bears witness to this. Despite my physical suffering and my despair over the face I had lost forever, I viewed the situation with some detachment and struggled for forgiveness to win out over hatred. I sought to understand rather than to take drastic action. I took into account the pathological nature of jealousy, which gives rise to uncontrollable impulses. Not only did I not wish death on the man who had nearly caused mine, but I feared that he would put an end to his life when he realized what he had done.

What is more, as soon as my husband gave himself up to the police I made it known to the judges, as I said, that I gave him my total pardon. I found excuses for him, stressing that he would never have acted like that in his normal state. I knew that Rachid risked ten years in prison and as many as 300 lashes in a public place. When I thought of the effect this would have on my children, my blood froze. My intervention allowed the sentence to be reduced to six months in prison, still with the 300 lashes, although these would be given "in private," I was assured. This was still too much. I made further efforts to defend Rachid, to the point that a judge said to me: "But come, madam, we are not going to acquit him after what he did?"

I wanted to say yes, but I didn't go that far. Finally, Rachid was spared the lash and sentenced to only three months in prison. Thanks to me, he got off lightly.

That said, I got something in return from my husband. I made a deal with the judiciary: in exchange for pardoning him, I got custody of my children for life. They wouldn't return to their father at the age of eight, as laid down in Qur'anic law, applicable to all divorced parents. This was, for me, the most important aspect of the case; such a custody deal was not easy to obtain, so strong is the image of the all-powerful father in our country. I had to fight hard for it, but it was an enormous relief. What would the lash have brought me compared to the happiness of being able to ensure that my children were educated according to my standards? That brought me much more than knowing that my husband was being punished.

My husband's family didn't let me down. They remained at my side throughout the whole experience, unable to do enough to be nice to me, to lessen my suffering and try to make me forget Rachid's crazed act, continually thanking me for my generosity toward him. I still correspond regularly with his sister, who lives in Lebanon. Very strong ties of friendship were created after this drama because I was determined to respect the father of my children. His family was grateful to me.

But what I underwent marked me for life, physically and emotionally. When my husband was released, for example, I feared he was going to come and hit me again, when in fact he had peaceably withdrawn to one of his sisters. But there was nothing I could do to stop such feelings. I was frightened at night. Three times I called the police, having heard noises and believing that someone had gotten into my house. Very kindly, the police came and, of course, found no one. What is more, each time one of them stayed on sentry duty outside my house until morning to reassure me. When I woke up, I was filled with shame, but my kind guards never held my anxieties against me; on the contrary, they have since gotten into the habit of calling me every night to make sure that everything is all right. Their solicitude touches me and I make it a point of honor not to disturb them anymore. At a time when I am sought from all sides to take part in conferences with organizations that defend women's rights, I think of their kindness and devotion. They remind me not to generalize about men. My actions must be precisely targeted and I must not be blinded by simplistic arguments, but instead define my priorities properly, as I did after my attack.

That is why I was attracted by the invitation from the French organization *Ni putes, ni soumises*, because I would be able to denounce what was happening not only in my country but in others and offer proposals to improve the situation. I am committed to be part of the wind of change that is finally blowing through the Arab world.

At present, change is coming mainly from Bahrain and Kuwait. On May 16, 2005, with the help of an amendment to electoral law passed by their parliament, Kuwaiti women obtained the right to vote and to run for parliament, despite the fierce opposition of Islamic and tribal MPs. The fact that a month later, on June 20, the first female minister, Maasuma al-Mubarak, took the oath in front of the assembly (to the boos of the extremist members), proved that while the battle is far from won, a great step has been taken.

Certain women in the Arab world have also subsequently shown their ministerial ambitions. Some of our leaders are favorable to this development and others are resistant, but sooner or later women will have to be admitted to their ranks. For too long, the government has relegated women to the sidelines, outside the main corridors of power; it is high time to introduce the necessary reforms.

At the last municipal elections in spring 2005, Saudi women believed they would finally be able to vote. It had been planned and agreed upon. The vote was without great political significance, but, even so, at the last minute everything was reversed: the authorities blocked the vote.

The government has, however, recently introduced a "council for dialogue." Composed of ministers, members of parliament, intellectuals, journalists, and scientists, its mission is to address the country's societal problems and the aspirations of its people. Allowing women to drive is the first great issue for these wise minds to debate.

Such a right is not a luxury. The unjustified discriminations that we undergo daily are revolting and have nothing to do with Islam. I don't see why on earth we cannot get an identity card or a passport without our husband's or father's agreement—the signature of one of these two men must appear on these documents... It is humiliating!

Women are nothing and everywhere men dominate. Even if women are given a starring role in our popular folktales, we do not exist in reality; we are only the shadows of our fathers, brothers, and husbands. It is appalling to realize that in Saudi Arabia a woman cannot walk down the street without men staring at her openly. For them, she is nothing but a body without a mind, something that moves and does not think. Women are banned from studying law, from civil engineering, and from the sacrosanct area of oil. Many jobs are forbidden to them, as are the ministries of industry, foreign affairs, energy, and transportation.

These bans exasperate me, but they do not affect my love of my country. I am proud of the courage and generosity of the Bedouins who track across the golden sands of the desert. There is no pollution between the sea and the dunes. I even miss the bitter taste of our coffee when I leave Jeddah.

For since my photos have been seen across the world, and since becoming an itinerant ambassador for Muslim women, my horizons have widened. My travels enrich me and open my eyes to the world, teaching me to see it differently.

In going to the different countries of the Maghreb—Tunisia, Algeria, and particularly Morocco, where I am regularly asked to take part in conferences—I have seen and admired the marvelous work that the Muslim women in these countries accomplish. Just like me, they respect Islam deeply but they fight daily for it not to diminish their freedom. Their work is courageous, for these women are known and pointed at wherever they go. Despite this, they continue to fight alone without the official support of the authorities. Kudos to them! I am in a good position to know the risks they run.

I am a disruptive presence because I give women ideas—my mother is the living proof of this. After years of marriage to my father, she has just broken her chains; no longer tolerating his authority, she has asked for and obtained a divorce. I would never have imagined it, so sealed did my mother's fate and her resignation to it seem. If she has protested, others will follow. And I will continue to fight for them, whatever happens.

As for me, I am savoring my new liberty. I am financially secure and since my divorce haven't had any money worries. I now have a fixed salary that allows me to bring up my children and even to treat myself to a chauffeur! I have also been contacted by an American television channel that broadcasts programs in Arabic.

But it isn't all roses. I am still benefiting from the shock waves caused by my attack, but for how long? What will happen to me when this is all forgotten? If I disappear into the shadows, some people may take advantage of my obscurity to make me pay dearly for my present audacity. That is why we must act now. We must quickly identify those who are distorting Islam in order to impose their own laws on women.

In the trials that I have been through, I have never given in to despair but have been able to remain optimistic. Books, my studies, and my contribution to various social projects have taught me a lot. Women must fight to improve their condition. Today I live alone with my children but I am free. After three decades of living, I have finally become an adult—and too bad if some people reject me.

Those who love God know the boundaries of what is forbidden. They do not need anyone to fix those limits for them.

Epilogue

I don't know if this chapter of my life is the beginning or the end, but I do know that my going to work in France was the first decision I made with total freedom of will. And for the first time I was able to smell the scent of freedom, a scent like jasmine one could fall in love with and get addicted to. In Paris, I made peace with myself and the simplest of things gave me pleasure. But activists like me are always in a state of war with the place, or with time, or even with people. In France, in the beginning, I suffered from being away from my children. I then moved to Lebanon so that we could be reunited. The day-to-day routine of life in France is difficult for single mothers. Believe it or not, when it comes to single mothers, the Arab countries are far better: there is greater societal support and more services. And, it is cheaper.

I chose Lebanon in particular because it is fertile territory for journalism and media. I was able to find work at al-Moustakbal Television (Future TV). There, I now have my own program called *Safahaat Khaleejiya* (Pages from the Arabian Gulf), a political news magazine that discusses issues relating to the region. But though I have gotten used to many things, there are still challenges.

Four long years have passed and I am still unable to bring my daughter from my first marriage to live with me; I cannot even visit with her. She has grown so much and she has become beautiful. She would prefer to live with me, and as for me, my life without her has no meaning. I kiss every piece of mail I send to her from Lebanon. I think about her every night and how I might bring her to Lebanon. I constantly think of ways to free her from her father. Yes, I have been turned into a criminal. At these moments, I've come to understand completely why a cat would eat her kittens when danger approaches.

As for love, I surely didn't get any because I didn't see it. Perhaps I was blind. It is possible that I loved for hours, maybe months, but I was aware that it wasn't love but something that resembled love.

The real achievement is my mother. She divorced my father and later remarried. She managed to overcome her fear of him. But my father poured all his anger on me and severed all contact with me. Convinced that I was the cause of their divorce, he blamed me for everything. The truth, however, is that I am innocent. All I did was to offer my mother the choice to come live with me.

Happiness—and sadness—is life; and we are the ones who make life what it is. I am not sad because of what happened to my face, because if it weren't for that I would not have come to know the taste of freedom. And I would not today be involved in the many important causes and in the planning of important projects in my life such as the building of a safe house for battered women in need. This is my real dream.

My family remains my support system. My brother has now become a man and today he looks after all our interests. He is the only fair-minded and reasonable man in our lives, someone who will always be there for me and my mother and my sisters. The young have now grown up and they have dreams that I hope they will have the ability to fulfill. As for my father, he has lost us all. To this day, he is unable to understand what it means to be a woman living in a society where customs and traditions—even your man— are against you. Even my little sisters started rebelling and I am sure that they will follow their own paths. Wherever their path may lead them, they will always remember what I have done.